The Tao of Allowing

Surfing on the Law of Attraction

By GP Walsh

Published by GP Media, LLC

Dear ZAy
Allow all goodness & love to
Come to you in abundance

Copyright Notice

GP Media LLC

7135 Collins Av Suite 1105

Miami Beach, FL 33141

Phone: 305-517-7610

Email: inquiries@gpmediallc.com

Edited by Tara King

Audio Book recorded at Ellis Island Studio - Miami, FL.

Sound editing by David Ellis

Diagrams created using Simple Diagram 2

If you have a moment, would you please be so kind to leave a review on Amazon.com? All my books are works in progress. I am always looking for ways to make them more relevant and clear to my readers.

I am not really in the business of writing or promoting books. I am in the business of helping people lead fuller, richer lives. So I need to know what you think. What worked for you, and, what did not? What was crystal clear, and, what was clear as mud?

So, thank you for downloading this book and please let me (and the rest of the known world) know how you felt about it.

GP

"Stillness and tranquility set things in order in the universe." - Lao Tzu

Dedication

To my love, my life partner, my mentor and my best buddy Mabel

Contents

Foreword

By Christy Whitman - New York Times Bestselling Author

When I first appeared as a guest on his radio show, I knew within the first few minutes of talking with G that he and I shared a fundamental belief: the "secret" to using the laws of deliberate creation to more easily manifest our desires goes much deeper than visualizing and wishful thinking. As someone who has spent the past two decades studying, applying and teaching others how activating universal principles such as intention, attraction, detachment, polarity and allowing can generate mind-blowing, measurable changes in our lives, I've come across a lot of books that merely skim the surface when it comes to explaining exactly *how* to harness these powerful forces to create more of what we want. This is not one of those books.

A key piece of the manifestation puzzle that is often overlooked – and is addressed head-on in this work – is that before we can successfully take that next step toward greater fulfillment, abundance and success, we must feel in the very core of our being and nervous system that it is safe to take that step. As long as we are operating in a state of fear – whether expressed as resistance, defensiveness, or what G calls the "contrived, artificial behaviors" that we adapted early in life to ensure our continued acceptance in our social "tribe" – all our efforts forward inevitably grind to a halt, every single time. The experience that I hear from many of my coaching clients when we first begin our work together is one of wanting to become more self-expressed and fulfilled in some key area of their lives, but feeling as through something is blocking them. While they define the problem perfectly, the solution doesn't lie in pushing ourselves to take more and more external actions, but in learning to release the brakes that are holding us back from within.

The Tao of Allowing speaks to the very issue of what causes us to resist our own desires, and what allows us to release that resistance, in a way that I believe many will be able to hear. It is not a superficial approach that advocates simply affirming our way to greater happiness. Anyone who has tried this knows that it has limited success. Yes, we may be able to find and stay in our "happy place" for a short period of time, but the moment we hit a bump in the road, the self-limiting core beliefs that our positive thinking pressed into hiding are jarred back to the forefront of our minds, causing us to lose both focus and traction. That this book can effectively guide readers into a greater state of allowing is because it is not a collection of feel-good techniques but rather a practical training system which methodically reprograms the nervous system – not to suppress uncomfortable feelings, but to embrace discomfort as part of the process of our evolution.

Immersed as we are in a culture that idolizes high achievement and overnight success, we often fail to recognize that in order to evolve any part of our lives beyond what they are in this moment requires us to feel some degree of discomfort. It's simply not possible to grow into more of who and what we want to become while remaining perfectly comfortable, because the moment we ask for more (and as long as we are alive and breathing, we never stop asking for more!), we trigger long hidden conditioned patterns of thought that tell us we can't have it. While some Law of Attraction guides would advocate visualizing or affirming our way through this discomfort, G and I are aligned in the conviction that these feelings hold the key to manifesting what we desire; literally providing a road map of the inner changes we must make in order to steer our outer lives in a new and more fulfilling direction. In his down to earth, honest, and sometimes irreverent style, G shows readers how to recognize the specific ways that resistance manifests itself in our bodies, emotions, thoughts and beliefs – all of which combine to create our dominant state of being, and our point of attraction.

Every so-called "negative" feeling is simply an outdated strategy once employed to help keep us safe. As we learn to let these feelings be instead of fighting against them – to feel them and allow them to exist even as we continue moving in our desired direction – we literally reprogram the way we respond to Life. Like a newborn baby deer wobbling on stick-thin legs, we keep on taking one step after another, building confidence, trust, and safety with each one.   Cultivating the inner knowing that it is safe to take the next step toward success is the very key that opens the door that allows more success into our lives. The door unlocks from the inside out; not the other way around. As we teach our nervous system, once exclusively committed to our survival, that it's safe for us to be as successful, as wildly abundant, as brilliant, and as outrageously happy as we desire to be, it drops all its defenses and eagerly and excitedly allows these experiences to come into our lives. When an outer opportunity arises, we meet it with an inner willingness to step up, charge ahead, and transform our intentions into reality.   Seeing the external manifestation of our inner desires is one of the most exhilarating experiences we have the honor to experience as human beings, and I wish it for each and every one of you!

Christy Whitman
Vancouver, B.C.
Fall, 2013

Acknowledgements

Writing a book was one of the most difficult things I have ever done. Even though i write a lot, actually organizing my normal extemporaneous talks into a coherent flow that would resemble a book was daunting.

I want to thank my editor Tara King for her expert guidance and suggestions (not to mention her blunt criticism). I want to thank my sons Gregory and Chris for being a constant reminder that legacy matters and that what little I may have to contribute to the alleviation of suffering should be set down for others to benefit. (And also for running our company while I do all this spiritual stuff). Lillian Diaz and Vlady Gonzales who own the Juice and Cafe Bar who let me spend several hours a day, sitting n a beautiful place for just the cost of a couple of cups of tea. Stop in and get a great fresh juice or cafe con léche when you are in Miami Beach at 7111 Collins Av.

I also want to thank my amazing friend John Kling for his untiring support, his willingness to read whatever I wrote and his unbelievable ability to find every mistake in punctuation. Evan Gregor for showing me that the next generation needs the guidance of us old guys and their willingness to receive it. All the members of The Balls Project forum for their inspiring dedication to 'Allowing' and willingness to be true to genuine manhood. All of my students who constantly uplift me and make me realize this is all worth it. All of the people all over the world who are doing "Allowing' as a regular practice and changing the energy of the whole world.

And thanks to my beautiful wife Mabel, who after 35 books of her own was patient with me as I struggled with my first.

Preface

Be the stream of the universe!

Being the stream of the universe,

Ever true and unanswering

Become a little child once more.

- Lao Tsu

I wish I had a dime for every time I have heard a Law of Attraction guru say, "you have to allow it", or, "practice the art of allowing", or, my personal favorite, "you aren't vibrating in harmony with the thing you desire."

Duh! Ya think?

Stating the obvious isn't helpful. How does one *allow*? That is the question.

After hearing those kinds of statements enough times that I could actually mouth the words while they were being said, (and sometimes, even before they were said), it became clear to me what I needed to do.

Explain!

> *"If you go looking for a book you really*
> *need and can't find it, it probably*
> *means you are the one who is supposed*
> *to write that book." - Unknown*

After almost 40 years of practicing, and almost that much time teaching everything from metaphysical prayer (prayers of affirmation), meditation, self-inquiry, and just about every self-help technique under the sun, I can say with a great deal of certainty that there **is** a way to learn how to allow all the goodness and power and self-expression into your life.

This book is a heartfelt attempt to bridge that gap between necessity and ability, and to guide the aspiring Law of Attraction student, step-by-step, into the mastery of this subtle and totally misunderstood practice.

Introduction

Your life isn't working. You don't like yourself. You want to be happy, healthy, wealthy, and all the other things that the Law of Attraction crowd have been pitching.

But, it ain't happening, is it?

What if I could show you why it hasn't been working, and why it is way easier than you thought to make it happen?

What if I could show you how to lose the struggle you have with your life, and lose it for good?

What if I could help you get to all those fundamental inner blocks that have kept you from realizing all these great promises and *remove them permanently?*

What if I could do that in about 20 minutes a day... starting today?

Would that be of interest to you?

I thought so!

I am going to share with you how to awaken to the magic of 'allowing', and how *that* is the real activating principle behind this thing that has come to be called, the Law of Attraction.

In fact, I have been doing this for people for a long time now ... long before there were coaches, long before there was a "Secret", and certainly long before almost all this self-help stuff even existed. Believe it or not, there was a time when all the self-help books in print didn't fill a single shelf in the bookstore.

By the time you finish reading this book, you are going to understand perfectly what has actually been holding you back. You will finally understand the real reason you have not experienced the great promise that all those self-help teachers speak about. After this, you will not need to run around looking for the perfect technique or teaching anymore. You will be able to jump off the self-improvement treadmill for good.

Instead, you will experience an inner joy, contentment, composure, and unshakable *feeling* of success that will transform every single interaction you have with every single person, plant, animal (and even every rock, bus, park bench, or shoelace) you meet.

Think I'm kidding? One guy I worked with said, "the whole world looked different. The colors were more vivid. It was like I was seeing through different eyes." Another guy remarked, "it was like 30 years of self-help teaching all made sense to me in a single moment."

A lovely British lady volunteered this feedback, "I couldn't believe it. Timid me, standing there completely unaffected by the big man yelling at me. I just allowed his anger and bullying to pass right through me. Later, he even gave me the very thing I had asked for, that had caused him to go off in the first place."

"It's easier to ride a horse in the direction it's going." - Old Zen Saying

The keyword in all this is **'ALLOWING'.** You can think of it as surfing the wave in the direction it is headed. Obvious, but, believe it or not, without even realizing it, you have been doing the exact opposite.

I promise you that I will give you everything you need to understand how this works, and how to start making it work for you. Like I said, this is *not* rocket science. I am going to show you how to 'allow' your natural resources, creativity, and resilience, to totally take over your life so that it flows as smoothly as hot chocolate sauce over your favorite ice cream.

I must warn you however, that this is a *training*. It is not a seminar. It is not a technique, or a bunch of pretty thoughts. I can only compare the training to that of learning how to ride a bike for the first time. You get on the bike and start to ride, but, of course, you fall over. You get back on again and ride, but again, fall over. This process continues, until suddenly, through the magic of the very nature of your own nervous system, you have mastered bike riding. All the while, I will be like your mom or dad holding you up as you learn (or rather, as your body learns) how to balance yourself and keep yourself upright.

> **"You can practice shooting eight hours a day, but if your technique is wrong, then all you become is very good at shooting the wrong way." - Michael Jordan**

'Allowing' is the flow. 'Allowing' is the magic of life. 'Allowing' is the path I am inviting you to walk. 'Allowing' is the Tao.

I cannot emphasize enough that this is a **training**, not a magic pill, or some kind of quick fix. You have to do it, do it some more, do it again, and then do it over again. Then, when you are too tired to do anything at all, you do it again! The things that have kept you from being, doing, and having everything you want to be, do, and have, have been installed as pre-programmed responses in your nervous system. So they act automatically. They will not just disappear because you get some great insight from a book or a class, or because you have that big ah-ha moment on a weekend retreat. Your system needs to be retrained.

This book is the start of your training.

Imagine what your life would be like if *everything* was easy. Struggle was all but removed and even hard times (yes there will always be hard times) are met with inner strength, resilience, patience, and a deep faith that "I am equal to this."

Before I proceed further, I need you to understand that I am NOT promising any of that get-rich, get-enlightened, get-happy-instantly, nonsense. Instead, what I am offering is the chance to enjoy unrestricted access to all those natural inner resources (which you already have by the way) that are equal to whatever comes along in your life.

What becomes awakened within you is your natural confidence, your natural capacity to respond rather than react. You find yourself slow to anger. You find it easy to understand even complex events and people. You are willing to wait for a good solution rather than feeling a need to make something happen. You enjoy more and struggle less.

In short, you feel powerful, but not in the way we normally think of it. It is a quiet power, a natural authority. Suddenly, without having to manufacture it, you find that you are imperturbable. You just KNOW that there is nothing that can happen in your life that you can't deal with effectively, calmly and for the benefit of all.

What about that? Would that be OK?

That is better than wealth, better than success, better than any accomplishment, even better than any relationship. It is better than anything you can acquire. Why? Well, any acquisition can be lost. Inner resources, on the other hand, can never be lost once they have discovered. They are yours forever.

Now, *that* is a treasure worth seeking.

Chapter 1
How I Came To Know And Allow...

"Creativity is allowing yourself to make mistakes. Art is knowing which ones to keep."
- Scott Adams

I have done many things in my life. Like you, I enjoy applying myself, and I like being successful. I have been successful in everything from software and entrepreneurship, to music and composition, to voiceovers for radio, TV, and even video games. I have been successful as a coach in both the professional and personal field, as well as a consultant to a number of fortune 500 companies. I have also excelled as an Information Systems Architect, a spiritual teacher, a meditation master, and, most importantly, as a father.

Mind you, I have experienced enormous failures as well. Success did not come easy to me. My family was not successful at anything. In fact, they had a decided lack of ambition, and were not even interested in much outside of watching TV and complaining. So I had to learn this all on my own. Most importantly for you, the reader, is that I have actually done all the things I teach in this book. I had to learn The 'Tao of Allowing', first hand!

In my book, "Original Innocence", I delve into great detail of the personal experience that first opened my eyes to the 'Tao Of Allowing', however, I will offer a little thumbnail of that momentous moment here.

Growing up in a very dysfunctional family, headed by an emotional and psychologically disturbed mother and an almost absent father totally lacking in ambition, I never really knew love or safety. I was a guest in the house and I was told that directly and unambiguously.

By the age of twelve, I was out on the streets every night, getting into trouble, doing my best to quiet the enormous amount of pain that was my everyday experience.

My natural gift for music was what saved me. I had started when I was five years old and loved it. It came very easily to me, both in my capacity as an instrumentalist and as a singer. The last thing my parents wanted, however, was a musician, so it was another point of contention and constant discouragement.

Fortunately for me, the 60s was the era of true rock n' roll, and this was precisely where I found my perfect fit. I spent all of my time either playing music, listening to music, or talking about music. While there was no doubt the power of song had become my saving grace, it brought with it a dark side.

I was not immune from the lure of the hippie life, and so, when I was around fifteen years old, I started doing drugs. At first, it was an enormous relief. It gave me a temporary rest from the pain and anxiety which were my normal state.

But what positive effects there were soon wore thin, and I found myself even worse off than before. The high and its attending relief got harder and harder to come by and so the drugs got increasingly severe and strong. Uppers, downers, hallucinogenics, speed, hashish. I would try anything. But to no avail. I was not only feeling the constant sense of deprivation and anxiousness, now I was addicted.

By the time I was nineteen, I was a pretty big mess, but I was slowly beginning to realize it. I longed to be free of it and make something of my life but I had no idea how. I had no example of that in my family, and as for my peers, well they were just like me. My rock star idols meanwhile, though genuinely great musicians, were horrible role models. I had no one to look up to.

Following high school, I tried college but dropped out soon after. I just couldn't keep up, concentrate, or even show up to class. I worked odd jobs, played in bands and generally scraped by. My family didn't have any money so I was pretty much on my own.

In the summer of 1971, I took a gig with a bar band in Wisconsin. The legal drinking age in that state was 18 for beer, and so, all over the state, there were these beer bars, especially in college towns. With everything I owned sitting in the back seat of a Rambler American, I headed off to lead the rock n' roll life. In short, I lived in a house with my fellow band members, played gigs, and got stoned.

On one particular night, after getting high with a bunch of people, I had the most horrible experience I had ever known.

A terror came over me that is impossible to describe. My throat tightened to the point where I was wheezing. I could barely breathe. My heart was pounding out of my chest. My head was throbbing and I was paralyzed. I couldn't move, couldn't speak, couldn't interact. My life passed before me and I thought I was dying. Frankly, I would have welcomed it.

Suddenly, and without any act of will on my part, my body got up, walked out the door and just kept walking. It was terrifying to be so out of control but, strangely, it was also a kind of relief. But it didn't matter how I felt about it, I had no control. I was on autopilot.

I walked for about thirty or forty minutes when, just as suddenly as it had started, the walking stopped. I turned right and found myself standing on a bridge looking down into a smelly, polluted river.

It was at that point that I broke down. I began to rant, vent, and cry as all my self-hatred and self-loathing poured out of me. I hated the world and what it had done to this, now almost dead river. I hated myself for what I had done to me. There was no relief. I was a bottomless pit of pain, anger, disillusionment, and hopelessness.

In the midst of this explosion I heard a voice. It was so powerful and authoritative that it stopped me in my tracks. It said, "look closer."

I obeyed. I stared down into the ugly, murky water. "What am I looking for?"

"Look closer. Look REALLY close!"

I put all my focus and energy on this water and suddenly found myself shrinking. Shrinking and falling. I was in the water getting smaller and smaller until I was just surrounded by blackness, suspended in space. I was so small that all around me I could see the molecules that made up the river.

"Look at the water" the voice said.

At this size I could see the water molecules and the molecules of the various pollutants.

"The water and the pollution haven't bonded, have they?" the voice continued.

It was true, from this vantage point there as a clear distance between the two. They weren't even touching.

"And if you could find a process to separate them, you would have the same pure, pristine water you always had, wouldn't you?" the voice asked.

"Yes, you would," I answered. "It would be the same water it always was."

Then, the voice said, "Greg, that's you!"

It was as though someone had torn open the top of my head and poured in an abundance of light. I was filled with an almost unbearable clarity and peace.

The next thing I knew, I was standing on the bridge again. All the effects of the drug had vanished. My heart had stopped pounding, my throat had opened, and I was breathing normally.

My mind was clear. My heart was at peace and, for the first time in my life, I felt loved.

That discovery happened spontaneously and dramatically, however, while making a significant discovery is one thing, integrating it into one's life is a different story altogether.

When the Wright Brothers made the first powered flight over one hundred years ago, it was a really big deal. The Aviation Age had come. What most people don't realize however is that it took several years for that great event to come to fruition. It was at least a further three years before they were able to make an airplane that did anything useful.

The actual victory of flight was a novelty. Before aviation could really be introduced to the world, they had to make an airplane that flew high enough, fast enough, long enough, and could carry enough weight. Needless to say, those advances and improvements did not happen overnight. As with everything, time, patience, and persistence was absolutely crucial.

And so it was for me. Realizing that the purity of my soul (and yours) was still intact, and had never been touched, was the first step. As the voice had said, a process needed to be found that could separate the pure, original you, from the pollutants.

Through many, many trials, experiments, grand successes and abject failures, I eventually began to understand how this all works. How our identities get formed. How our dysfunctional and sometimes destructive habits get put into place.

Eventually, I discovered just how to separate the pollutants from the pure you.

What I found is that it all starts with The 'Tao Of Allowing', and the results I experienced were conclusive: *When I worked with life, my life worked. When I worked against it, it didn't.*

Always remember that.

Chapter 2
Why Do They Keep
Saying, 'Allowing'?

"The journey from teaching about love to allowing myself to be loved proved much longer than I realized." - Henri Nouwen

Question: What is the single most important element when it comes to achieving results from all your self-help work, including personal development techniques, spirituality, Law of Attraction, Meridian Tapping, NLP, meditation, all of it?

Answer: Allowing!

"Why 'allowing'?" you might ask. "I thought it was visualization, consistently holding positive thoughts, and raising my vibrational set point?"

Well that is all good stuff, but...

Let me ask you another question. Would you stand in the ocean and try to push the waves back out to sea? Would you stand there defiantly, armed with all your self-empowerment knowledge, all those good thoughts, all the while being continuously (and unceremoniously) knocked on your butt?

Of course, you wouldn't!

That would be really, really stupid. I mean, nobody in their right mind would do that. Oops, sorry, but that is *exactly* what you have been doing!

You may, of course, have been just sitting there on your beach blanket wishing you could surf, perhaps, finding the whole thing a bit intimidating. You may have even abandoned your dream of surfing, and so, instead, you merely watch the wave rather than riding it. When Orville Wright was asked, "isn't flying dangerous?" he responded,

"Safe is sitting on the fence watching life go by!"

Now contrast that with the guy who breaks out his surfboard, waxes it up, paddles out a bit or maybe a lot, waits for the right wave, paddles like crazy to catch it, and then rides it to the shore. Then he does it again! Tell me, who understands the nature of a wave? The guy on the surfboard, or, the guy on the beach covered in SPF 100?

The Law Of Attraction IS The 'Tao Of Allowing'

The term Law of Attraction has entered into the popular vocabulary. My radio show is even syndicated through The Law of Attraction Radio Network. The term has tens of hundreds of thousands of searches on Google each month. Everybody knows the words. Almost nobody knows what it is.

The Law of Attraction is just a term we have invented that captures what is, in fact, simply the nature of life

Yes, the phenomena that was relatively recently named, the Law of Attraction is simply the natural way in which the energy of life flows. Practitioners of Chinese medicine, acupuncture, martial arts, yoga, chi gong, along with the Taoists, Buddhists, Hindus, and countless others, have known for thousands of years what appears to be a quite a mystery here in the west. It is nothing other than the way things work.

All of life works like those ocean waves. In this chapter, we are going to make sure that you clearly see that you have either been fighting the waves of your life, or, sitting on the shore of life watching them, instead of surfing. Then, I am going to show you where you left your surfboard and help you take your first surfing lesson.

"The Lady Doth Protest Too Much, Methinks"

"Hey, I am not fighting waves!" you respond, "That would be stupid! I am just trying to get ahead. I'm doing what it takes. I am working diligently to manifest my dream life! I have my vision board and my treasure map. I regularly have my Chakras cleaned, along with my colon! I meditate. I have binaural beats on my iPod. I even have a hundred thousand dollar bill taped to the ceiling above my bed. (Not a real one, of course.)"

Uh... sorry... but you are just fighting waves.

You know. I hear it all the time, "I feel stuck, pushed around, unable to get ahead, two steps forward, three steps back. Flat on my back again. Stuff just happens to me and I don't know why."

Or you may be a little more advanced and say, "It must my negative thinking and my unconscious patterns" or, my personal favorite, "I need a new technique"

And the most painful one of all, "I must not be doing it right."

If you don't think you are fighting life, then let me give you the litmus test. It is a very simple question. Do you feel like you are struggling?

Now, please do *not* give me any stories or explanations of how complex your circumstances are. Don't tell me stories about your childhood and your parents, or girlfriend/boyfriend who rejected you in 6th grade. We will get to those later. Right now, it is just a simple yes or no question. Right here. Right now. In this very moment.

Do you *feel* like you are struggling?

If feel you are struggling, then you are not in the Tao... period!

The only way you can possibly feel like you are struggling is that you are trying to push the waves back out to sea. Struggling is the clear indicator that you **are** fighting with the invisible wave of life. You are not surfing. Surfers don't struggle. They only steer. Folks, you are not surfing. Actually, you are not even swimming in the 'Tao Of Allowing'. You are either flat on your butt cursing the waves, or, you are sitting on your blanket watching... and yearning.

'Allowing' Is The Tao

The word Tao simply means *The Way*.

THE way, not A way.

It is not one of a large number of potential ways. It is THE way. Now, please understand. This is not some dogma or ideology. This is not some belief system. There is no Kool-Aid that you will be required to drink. It is the simple recognition of *how things are*. It is the bewilderingly simple acknowledgment that waves are to be surfed, not fought. Nor are they to be watched, passively, from a distant vantage point.

If you have been doing any kind of personal growth work that involves this idea of the Law of Attraction, then you have undoubtedly heard the word 'allowing'. Do you have any idea what it really means? I mean all the Law of Attraction teachers preach its virtue. Maybe you have even been told to 'allow' by a Success Coach, or a Manifestation Coach, or a friend trying to be helpful. The dialog goes something like this:

> **You:** I have done the visualizations, all the exercises, the vision board, the mind movies, the binaural beats and self-hypnosis, all of it.

So, why am I still not manifesting at the level I want

Guru: You need to allow.

You: Ah, yeah... that's it... I get it. OK, I'll do that. I am going to allow all that stuff to just come flowing into my life.

...three months later

You: Excuse me, but I'm still not manifesting that big dream.

Guru: You need to 'allow'... some more.

You: Huh? I thought I was! I mean what have I been doing for the last 3 months?

Guru: Obviously you haven't been, or you would be getting the results. Try 'allowing' some more.

You: ARRRRRRRRRRG

Not a particularly helpful dialog is it? But the guru is right. You do need to learn to 'Allow'.

But (and this is a big but) 'allowing' is not a skill. It is a **Way of Life**. Actually, it is **THE way of life**. It is not information you learn. It is a way of 'being' that you train yourself in. You don't force change to happen. You don't coax, coerce, or, seduce the Law

37

of Attraction into giving you what you want. That would be trying to push the waves out to sea. Instead, you 'Allow' things to change in a way that is in accord with their own nature. In other words, you surf. This is the 'Tao of Allowing'.

'Allowing' is not a skill. It is a way of life

It really couldn't get any simpler. You simply let things be as they actually are. What is so hard about that? I mean, what could possibly be hard about being what you already are? Even though it is simple, however, it is not easy. You will understand why by the time we are done.

Need A Better Hammer?

We all genuinely want to improve our lives. Wanting to be, do, and have more, is innate in us humans. We want to make things, experience things, and have things. We are naturally curious, creative, playful, and fun loving. Whenever our basic needs are taken care of, we immediately start looking for something interesting to do. We can't help it. We can't stop it. It is our nature.

So, when we learn of something like the Law of Attraction, we get really excited. I mean, wow! Everything I ever wanted to have, be, or do, I can? Right now? Of course, we want to experience that amazing promise. Once we come to feel, in our gut, that this is really true, it opens us up to possibilities we hadn't thought possible before that. It actually gets us dreaming again!

But, like that illusive mirage that never gets any closer, no matter how fast we run or drive, we are, for the most part, discouraged by the meager results that we have gotten. It feels more like a tease than a liberation, more like a cruel joke than a fulfilled promise.

It really is like salt being poured into the wound when we hear a Law of Attraction guru say, "you have to allow it into your life."

I mean, really! You wouldn't have read all the books you have read, done all the courses you have done, learned the techniques you have learned, if you were not totally sincere about attaining the life you know is possible. You wouldn't be reading this book right now either, if you weren't totally committed to doing what it takes. So willingness, sincerity, and, persistence, are NOT the problem. Hear this please:

> ***Your dedication and resolve
> are unquestionable. That is NOT
> the problem.***

So what is?

You don't need another technique. You don't need another book. You don't need another retreat. You already have all the information you need. The next technique is not going to work any better than the last one, because the problem isn't with the technique.

The problem isn't the hammer. You've simply been pounding on the wrong nail!

That is why you went to some event or read something inspiring, had the big ah-ha moment, only to return to your regular life, and have it all vaporize right in front of your eyes. If the answer was in a technique, you would have had it. Any hammer will pound the nail, so you don't need a different one. You just need to learn to swing it with authority and mastery, and, more importantly, land it on the right target.

Chapter 3
In The Beginning...
There Was 'Allowing'

"And I saw everything that I had made, and, behold, it was really good." - God

Have you ever met a young child that was **not** his or herself?

Children live constantly in the **'Tao Of Allowing'**. That does, of course, include you. You too were one of those children who lived in the natural flow of life without even having to think about it. As a matter of fact, you couldn't think about it. You couldn't think at all in the beginning, nor did you have to.

The Tribe

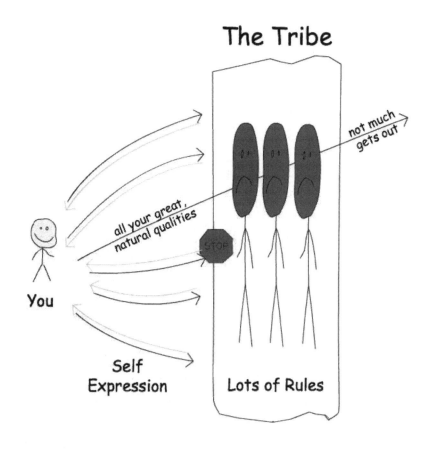

all your great, natural qualities

not much gets out

You

Self Expression

Lots of Rules

(Sometimes images don't display very well in a Kindle book. To download the image visit here http://JustAllowIt.net/TaoOfAllowing)

'Allowing' is our natural, original, state. Unfortunately, it gets trained out of us. Look at the diagram above. You start out just naturally expressing who you are, but who you are does not always conform to what your family and your culture find acceptable.

'The Law of Your Tribe of Origin' is what I call the sum total of all the rules, morals, codes of behavior, attitudes, definitions of what is acceptable, both spoken and unspoken.

It doesn't matter how natural your behavior is, if it is not acceptable for The Tribe, then you will have to get rid of it. Your survival depends on it.

But here is the rub. You *can't* get rid of it. It's you! It is what comes naturally. It's like asking a dog not to bark! You have to understand that, no matter how unacceptable it may have been to The Tribe, it is still you.

The message that is received loud and clear is that *you* are not acceptable. Whether it was intentional or not on the part of your parents, that is the message. You were too young to discern the difference between who you are and what you do. So, in order to protect you from rejection from The Tribe (which to the body means a death sentence), your nervous system kicks in with one of the most remarkable features of adaptability ever created. We couch it in rather negative terms, but it is, in fact, a remarkable ability we all possess.

It is called **suppression**.

Suppression is the unique ability we all have that allows us to stop any behavior, even natural ones (and, in the beginning they are all natural) before they ever get out, and replace it with behavior that is acceptable to The Tribe. That is, behavior that will keep you safe. What does get out and get expressed, and most of it is an act, will become integrated into your sense of identity and ends up being a permanent part of your adult personality. Depending on how much of the real you is allowed expression, you may actually experience some degree of authenticity, but it will never be complete, and I do mean never.

You Want Some Proof?

A friend of mine told me of an experience she had when she was visiting her sister and her young daughter. The little girl was about two years old at the time. One day, the little one reached out to grab something she wanted. It really wouldn't have been a good thing for her to have, and so, her mommy shouted out a loud, "no!" and gave her a gentle slap on the wrist.

Not a violent slap mind you, just a little tap. Nonetheless, it wasn't much later when the curious little girl was reaching for something else. When she looked and noticed that both her mother and her aunt were looking at her, she stopped and *slapped her own wrist!*

My friend and her sister looked at each other in a combination of horror and amazement. They ran over to the little angel, and told her was okay. They tried their best to make amends. Now, mom is not a bad parent. In fact, she is an excellent mom. I did the same kind of thing when my kids were little, but just consider this. The child is not even two years old and already she is administering self-editing and self-punishment. The influence of The Tribe is subtle and absolute.

The little girl's nervous system has responded to the law of suppression, and she learned in a very real way, a very powerful lesson.

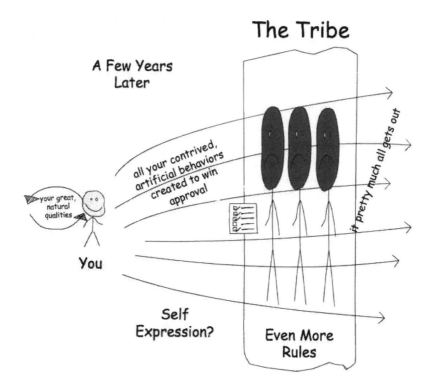

(Sometimes images don't display very well in a Kindle book. To download the image visit here http://JustAllowIt.net/TaoOfAllowing)

Actually the word "learn" is inaccurate. We don't learn to do this. It happens automatically. The system knows how to do this without learning. It simply responds to the environment, and creates what I call *"energetic assumptions."* Patterns of reaction that assume certain things about reality. The reality, for the youngster, of course, is The Tribe.

The energetic assumption was created, that curiosity, is dangerous. This same scenario has happened to all of us. No one is exempt. What results? Well, this does...

Instead of the natural expression of who you are, you create a bunch of contrived, artificial behaviors, that will guarantee you approval from The Tribe. The approval of The Tribe is what we need in order to feel safe, and so, in order to get this approval, behavior must first conform to The Law of the Tribe.

Safety is all the little person wants, and the nervous system is willing to do, or sacrifice, anything to get it.

Is It Bleak, Or Just Nature?

I wish I could say that it is possible to raise children without any kind of conditioning, but, it isn't! After all, there are some things that really are dangerous, and children need to learn to fear and avoid them. The problem is that, much of the qualities we are taught to fear and avoid, are only fearful because The Tribe doesn't like them, and not because they are really are dangerous or worthy of our fear.

It is those qualities, which really make up the heart and soul of our individuality. When our genuine individuality is not allowed to be expressed, we experience dysfunction, limits, dissatisfaction.

In short, we suffer.

All Or Nothing

Children do not have a developed capacity to understand subtlety. Everything is very simple for them. It is impossible for them to separate their behavior from themselves. If the parent says, "that is a bad thing to do," the child hears, "you are bad." Mommy and daddy are infallible, and mommy and daddy are the key to survival, therefore, in the mind of a child they **must** be right. All their actions are right, loving, fair, and the truth.

"Mommy, daddy = good. Me = bad." This is the irresistible motivation behind the absolute necessity of abandoning any behavior that is not acceptable to your parents, who are nothing less than the god and goddess of our existence.

We assume that the behavior we are expressing is not "good," which is interpreted to mean who we are is not good.

We assume we are flawed and defective. The behavior must be contained and even abandoned, and then replaced with new, artificial behavior that fits the expectations, even if that behavior is contrary to everything we are.

This redefining of our behavior is the reason why self-discovery and personal development work is so difficult. I will explain that more when I delve into the discussion of resistance, but, suffice it to say now, any behavior, that is not acceptable, is not just inconvenient or inappropriate. It is *totally* unacceptable. For the little nervous system trying to survive, being unacceptable becomes a simple matter of life and death. To be acceptable means to survive. To not be acceptable means death. It IS that simple and it IS that severe.

So, even if the quality being expressed, really is the best part of you, it must be *dis-allowed.*

As I mentioned earlier, I have a natural gift for and interest in music. Not only did I quickly learn instruments, I had a beautiful boy soprano voice. Well, art was not something valued in our house. Artists were way outside the bounds of what was acceptable for a good, salt of the earth, Midwestern family.

Every time I would open my mouth to sing, Mom would have something else that needed doing. Even when others in the room were amazed, she would leave the room or diminish me and quickly move the subject elsewhere. Once she told me, "don't sing so high, it will wreck your voice." I could just feel her rejection.

Once, during a performance at school, when I was about nine, I had a solo. When I started to sing, the audience gasped, as it was not the level of performance that was expected from an average grade school in an average town. When I mentioned

49

the reaction to my mother, she replied, "No they didn't. Don't think that way." No compliment. No praise. Not even a smile. I was devastated; embarrassed for even having imagined that.

Even though I had been performing in front of audiences almost all my life and felt as comfortable on stage as I did off it, a consequence of my mother's rejection of my talent was that I just couldn't sing, nor could I think of myself as a singer. In fact, I didn't even like my voice at all. I hated hearing recordings of it.

As I began to discover how suppression worked, and how it literally shuts down our best characteristics, I slowly began to regain that territory. I was in my 40s before the trauma I had experienced about my voice was finally released and I could sing again. It was then that I discovered people loved the sound of my voice so much that, for a while, I made a living doing voiceovers for TV, radio, video games and even a telephone answering system!

One woman once said about me, "I could listen to him read from the phone book." I now do a weekly radio show, meditation recordings and audio classes. People find my voice soothing, relaxing and easy to learn from.

As it turns out, it was one of my greatest strengths that I was deprived of for 40 years. It was liberated by the understanding of how suppression works, and the magical 'Tao Of Allowing'.

'Allowing' is really the liberation of who you are. This liberation allows all the natural energy to flow out, but it is only because of that early training that we don't have immediate and constant access to it now as adults. Since that is not happening naturally and spontaneously anymore, we have to retrain ourselves. We have to learn to drop the self-imposed obstacles and let that original, innocent, expressive, creative, and hopelessly beautiful being come out and play.

By the way, that innocent, expressive, creative, and hopelessly beautiful being is you!

So how do we do that? The 'Tao Of Allowing'. We must 'Allow' it to come out. And how do we do that? We must make it safe for it to do so.

"When I finally saw the connection between how I grew up and the challenges in my life it blew my mind. Throughout my life I was the quiet, good girl, always accommodating, always mediating, never sharing my opinion or who I was. This helped me live in my family and get along, but when I started to become a woman, it ate at me, something was missing, I wanted so much more. This translated into a degree and then career as a sign language interpreter where I was always speaking for someone else, sharing someone else's views and

opinions and was forbidden (by nature of the work) to share my own!! How crazy is that?

Working with G and being exposed to his teachings, I started to listen to the voice inside. I started to listen to my body! What I got was a screaming and yearning for ME to come out. I took the leap and now I can see from the other side, what started with listening to that voice with the guidance of G, I am now 100% doing the work I love as a coach of women entrepreneurs on a mission (not interpreting). I accept challenges in my career like taking charge of a $2 million project, or teaching on stage in front of 100s of people. Only a few years ago I would have said no, I would have ignored the inner voice, I would have said, oh no, I can't do that. Here is the kicker...I am making way more money as I continue to say yes.

I love G and I always love how he makes the concepts that are so hard to grasp easy for us mere humans to understand." ~ Beth

Chapter 4
What Allowing Is NOT!

"There is man in his entirety, blaming his shoe when his foot is guilty." - Samuel Beckett, Waiting for Godot

The Tao of Allowing

Since I have started teaching 'allowing' as a practice, I have heard a lot of objections, questions, and enquiries about it, that indicated quite a bit of misunderstanding. So, before we proceed further into the training, I want to first answer some of the questions you may be asking.

- Allowing Is NOT Inaction

- Allowing Is NOT Resignation

- Allowing Is NOT Apathy

- Allowing Is NOT Sitting On Your Butt

- Allowing Is NOT Becoming A Doormat

- Allowing Is NOT Weakness

- Allowing Is NOT Waiting

- Allowing Is NOT Idle Dreaming, or, Wishful Thinking

The surfer doesn't dream about surfing, she does it, but she doesn't fight the waves. She rides them; she trains herself extremely well in order to be able to do that.

If you are trying to grow muscle mass and endurance, you lift really heavy weights. Now, the fact is, in real life, you almost never have to lift that much weight. You are creating reserve strength for when you need it, and you do that by lifting way more weight than you would normally have to.

That is exactly what the practice of 'allowing' is. You are entering into the State of Allowing to the exclusion of all else, not because you are going to stay there indefinitely, but because you need to be there in order to master it. Once you master it, you can move into it and out of it at will. That is the point.

There are times when we need to act decisively, and then there are other times when we need to simply wait until the right moment has arrived. You *must* be able to tell the difference between the two.

As I have said over and over in this book, everything in life has a natural flow to it. Everything has its natural energy pattern. Learning that pattern and working with it, is the very soul of the 'Tao Of Allowing'.

So you see, 'allowing' is NOT resignation or idleness. It is not sitting around waiting for something to happen. It is not allowing others to treat you badly or take advantage of you. That is inappropriate acquiescence, not 'allowing'.

Allowing is not INACTION. It is the WAY in which you respond

The Tao of Allowing

Allowing is not an action, but it is the way in which one acts. The paradox of 'allowing' is that you can 'allow' even when you are in the full throes of action. It is a constant, subtle response to the way things are. That means, not trying to make them other than what they are, or even whining about the way they are. No time is lost in whining, complaining, or, wishing they were different. Instead there is instant response.

Imagine a General on the battle field. A whole regiment of the opposing army suddenly appears in the distance, charging over a hill. The General cannot waste anytime grousing, "what the hey! They aren't supposed to be there." It is already too late for that. The General instead acts as he has been trained. He acts with no thought of what it *should* be but in response to what *it is*. That is the 'Tao Of Allowing'.

So do not be concerned that you are going to become a milquetoast. You're not. The incredible miracle of 'allowing' is that you become remarkably adept at responding to anything, and those responses are quick, measured, and almost always effective.

Once you realize that you are naturally and completely endowed with those kind of inner resources, you reach a state of pure peace and imperturbability. You become a master of life, a master of the Tao.

I 'Allowed' ...

"Around a year ago now, I began working with GP one-on-one, as well as doing the 'Just Allow It' course at the same time. In the beginning, my experience of 'allowing' was that it was both amazingly simple to do, and yet still somehow difficult because of the tendency that many of us have to overthink/resist. I remember doing the very first exercise and thinking "okay, I'm pretty sure I'm doing this right but I don't actually know...this just seems really simple but it has to be more difficult than this." For quite a while, I would fluctuate between continuing to be totally caught up in thoughts/story, and then having periods where I was just feeling what was there fully, and was able to focus and sustain my attention there.

The first breakthrough came when I was able to sustain my attention on the sense of the body, and also be okay with thoughts coming up. A key factor in this for me was realizing that having thoughts occur is not inherently a bad thing, it's what the mind is supposed to do. Where we are led astray is having a thought come up, latching on to it, and then having that turn into a chain of thoughts where you end up completely lost in it. This is how most people are living every day. So the key for me was to simultaneously allow the thoughts to come up instead of trying to completely not think, and, at the same time not latch on to the thoughts but instead watch as one random thought comes up, then falls away, then another, then it falls away, etc. In this place you are still being totally present, but you are simply feeling your body and noticing the thoughts happening instead of having a chain reaction of thoughts occurring.

The other breakthrough came once I began to allow so called 'negative' feelings. I no longer label them as negative, though obviously feeling some things is preferable to others. It's typically easy for us to fully experience the things that make us feel good, but, when it comes to feeling painful memories, emotions, sensations in our body, our habit is to run the other way as fast as possible. I eased into this by having painful emotions/feelings come up and being with them for just a few seconds in the beginning. That turned into a little longer each time until I could fully be with the pain as long as it needed to be expressed. Through practicing this, I have had some big releases take place that have ultimately resulted in me feeling lighter and healthier physically, emotionally, and mentally.

The beauty of 'allowing' is that it is our natural state, and so once we start practicing it, our system begins to intuitively understand that this state of allowing is much more preferable to the habitually ingrained state of resistance that most of humanity lives in, which results in life being more effortless, lighter, and freer."

~ Whit

Chapter 5
It's All About Safety

*"There is always safety in valor." - Ralph
Waldo Emerson*

Discerning the real nature of our learned behavior (suppression), and that the only motivation was safety, we can begin to create the safe space in which the genuine 'you' can come out and play. 'Allowing' is the exact opposite of suppression, and it too is totally inherent in the system. That means that the simple act of 'allowing' creates that safe space. And then a real miracle occurs.

The miracle of all of this, is that once you 'Allow' the real you to emerge, and the system knows that it is safe to do so, it drops the suppression as quickly as it created it.

The system reprograms itself. That is a frick'n, world class, miracle.

Really, that's it? That's all it takes? Yep, that's it. The entire suppression process depends upon the perceived truth that you are not safe. Break that down and accept that it is just not true, and the nervous system (which is what created all those behaviors) will automatically start the process of dropping the resistance programming.

It really does happen that easily. And the reason why? Because 'allowing' is your natural state.

The system knows how to get back to it, if you remove the suppression, acknowledge that it is all about safety and recognize that you are, in fact, safe.

> *If you convince the nervous system, that the things you are seeking to bring into your life will actually make it more safe, it drops its defenses*

"Oh, well why didn't you say so?" Yeah really, the transformation can be that total and that fast.

YOU Have To Become Safe

No, I do not mean you have to set up your whole life so everything is perfectly safe. Not only is that really difficult, it isn't even possible, and many people have wasted their lives along with dozens, if not hundreds, of opportunities looking for perfect, perpetual safety.

No, I mean you, yourself, have to become regarded as safe to your own nervous system. Believe me, when you first start this practice of 'allowing', it will not regard you as safe.

Why is that? Because you are not!

This is a hard one for most people to hear but you have become your own worst enemy. Even though we all have the best of intentions, we have, by our constant attempts at "self-improvement," inadvertently been doing to ourselves, exactly what was done to us as children. We have been trying to force our behavior to be something other than what it naturally is.

We have been doing to ourselves exactly what was done to us that created the artificial behaviors in the first place.

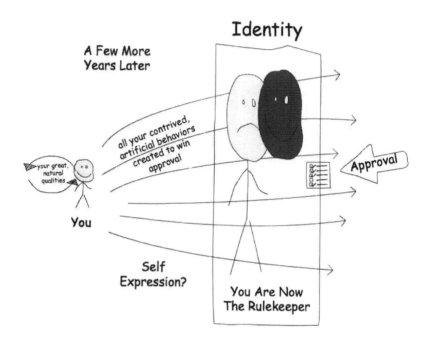

(Sometimes images don't display very well in a Kindle book. To download the image visit here http://JustAllowIt.net/TaoOfAllowing)

Our very attempts at "improving" ourselves have only driven the system deeper into defense. So, obviously, the only way to make it safe for the nervous system to drop its defenses is to demonstrate conclusively, that **you** can be trusted. You have to become a safe haven for your own body. And there is only one way to do this, self-acceptance.

The 'Tao Of Allowing' actually has a better name. Unconditional Love.

So, if you stick with this practice of 'allowing', just like riding a bike, your nervous system will take over and retrain itself. Your natural and totally sweet **State of Allowing** will emerge. It has actually been there all along. It's just that now, because you are creating the space, it is safe for it to come out.

The 'Tao Of Allowing'

The word Tao simply means the way, or, more figuratively, the way things are. The 'Tao of Allowing', or, the 'Way of Allowing', is nothing more than discovering the way things actually work, and then working with them *as they are*. To discover what something is and appreciating it for what it is, is unconditional love.

This is the Tao and it merits repeating:

To discover what something is, and appreciating it for what it is, is unconditional love

The Tao of Allowing

Imagine you have fallen into a rushing river. If you fight it, perhaps by grabbing on to a branch or a rock, you are going to get pummeled by the water rushing at you. You are going to get really beat up by all the rocks, sticks, and debris, being carried along by the rushing current.

Needless to say, it will not be a pleasant experience, and all of the visualization, positive thinking, and reframing, in the world is not going to change that. I mean, can the river change its nature? Can it stop rushing? Can it stop carrying along whatever falls into it? Would you really want it to?

But what if, instead, you simply let go? What if you just let yourself flow with the current, steering a little to avoid bumping into things but just going with the flow, as it were. Even though you could be rushing along at breakneck speed, the water around you would appear totally still. You and the river would be moving together. Its motion would become your motion. It would do all the work and your journey would be almost effortless.

This is the 'Tao of Allowing'.

Chapter 6
How To Allow! How To Get Safe!

"It's a very sobering feeling to be up in space and realize that one's safety factor was determined by the lowest bidder on a government contract. " - Alan Shepard

The Tao of Allowing

OK, so what is this thing called 'allowing', and, more importantly, how do I DO it? This thing you very well may have tried to DO, but have not been able to DO. I emphasized those words for a reason. OK, are you ready for the punch line?

Allowing isn't an ACTION - so you can't do it

That's a mind blower isn't it? I am pretty sure that this is a totally new concept for you, so let me explain.

We live in an action oriented culture. I don't care where you live, unless you are in an ashram, a monastery, or are an experienced Zen meditator, you are completely immersed in a culture that is totally about action. I mean, we have "Just Do It" emblazoned on our chests, for crying out loud! (And we paid $25 for the T-shirt, not to mention $200 for the shoes.)

The doer, the self-made man or woman, the movers and shakers, are our cultural ideal. They are downright archetypal. So it is only natural (or at least normal) for us to assume that the 'Tao Of Allowing' is some sort of action. It must be some kind of thing we DO, right?

Wrong. It isn't something you do. Allowing is a state, and it is a natural state at that.

So, What Is A State?

A state is a system at rest. It is the *potential* for action, but right at this moment, it isn't doing anything. When we are talking about an inner state we are referring to our *tendencies*, the way we *will* react to our environment. It is the way we were programmed to react to events as they happen in our lives.

> *A state is all the potential ways in which we will react to any event before the event has actually occurred*

Think of it like a computer. The computer doesn't do anything until it is told. It sits there idly until we tell it to do something. Not only that, but what it does is completely determined by the program that is loaded. It can't do anything other than what that program says to do. Even though the hardware *can* do any number of things, it *will* only do whatever the particular program dictates.

That is exactly how your nervous system works.

In other words, a state is our pre-programmed response to our own environment. If I am in a state of resistance, it means that the majority of my reactions to my environment will be resistant, protective, defensive. But if I am in the State of Allowing, all of my responses to events will be thoughtful, measured, intelligent, appropriate and full, with nothing held back. The State of Allowing is what Eckhart Tolle and Michael Brown call 'presence.'

The State We Are In, Determines Our Character

OK, so states are the potential for acting and the predefined way in which you will react when something happens. Since states comprise the sum total of how you behave in the world, taken together, they are nothing short of your character. When someone says, "he is so like that" (a statement often accompanied by a big roll of the eyes), or, "she always says that," they are referring to your dominant state, a.k.a your character.

Stop and ponder this for a moment, if you will. What others (and yourself as well) think of as *you*, is really just *the ways* in which you respond to the environment. Who you are is nothing other than the state of your nervous system.

Now, here is the kicker! For the most part, we don't have any control over these reactions. As I explained in the previous chapter, they were programmed into the nervous system as a survival strategy when we were still quite young, and they are still there waiting to be triggered. But (and this is a really big but), states CAN be reprogrammed. You can install a different set of software.

The Dominant State

We all have states which are our default. When you were growing up, there were certain behaviors that you had to exhibit in order to get the love, attention, and approval, you needed. Since that behavior (and all the thoughts, feelings, and attitudes, that go with it) had to be expressed spontaneously and consistently, it was programmed into the nervous system as the default or dominant state. Now remember what all the Law of Attraction people say. Whatever is the dominant vibration is what gets manifested in your life. The source of all the vibrations is your Dominant State. To put it in Law of Attraction terms,

The force that determines your vibrational set point is your dominant state

So, unless your dominant state is one of allowing, expectancy of good, self-acceptance, and an innate sense of safety, you are going to be pushing away the very things you want to have coming into your life. You will be pushing the waves back out to sea. Not only that, but you will do it automatically without even knowing you are doing it.

Sadly, for most of us, actually almost all of is, the dominant state is the State of Resistance. Don't believe me?

Stay tuned.

Chapter 7
Look Ma, No Hands

"Like a ten speed bicycle, most of us have gears we never use." - Charles M. Schulz

Remember when you were a kid learning to ride a bike? You got on and kept going until your **nervous system** figured out how to do it. By relentlessly attempting to ride the bike, your body got the message that this is what you wanted to have happen.

So, it dutifully began to "figure out" how to make that happen. It began to react to all the tiny, subtle cues that warned it of the possibilities that it could fall over. Since the body knows that falling over is not a good thing (it just knows, nobody had to tell it), eventually **IT** (the nervous system, not you) learned how to react to all that input from the environment in just the right way.

Your body was doing nothing other than seeking the safe state. It "knew" that falling over was dangerous, and that staying upright was safe, and so, it sought and found the safe state and made it automatic.

You didn't learn how to ride a bike. You just kept getting on the bike, and your body simply did the rest. You really didn't do anything at all except want to ride the bike and be willing to get on it over and over and over again until your body figured out how to keep you upright. Once that happened, it was party time, and it all became effortless!

What we experience as that exhilarating feeling of effortlessness is mastery.

EFFORTLESS = MASTERY

You probably haven't thought of yourself too often as a master. But you are. When any skill gets so well trained into the nervous system that we don't have to think about it anymore, we have become a master. Now let's take stock. You walk, talk, eat, scratch, run, dance, tie your shoes, get dressed, swing a hammer, use a telephone, a computer, household appliances, drive a car, the list is virtually endless. And you do all of those things without even thinking about it.

You are a master of life. You have entered into a State of Mastery in regards to so many aspects of your life. "Oh, all those everyday things? So what?" But the only reason you can call them everyday things is because you have mastered them! Now, of course, almost everybody has mastered those tasks so we don't make a big deal out of them, but that is precisely the point.

Anybody can master 'allowing', and, the 'Law of Attraction'!

When you were "learning" to ride a bike, your system was automatically responding to inputs from the environment in exactly the correct way. Once that state was established, you never had to think about it again. In fact, you couldn't forget how to do it if you tried.

The State of Allowing is just like that. You don't do it. You simply get on the Allowing bike and keep yourself there long enough for your body to figure out how to maintain the balance.

The State of Allowing happens
when you have sufficiently
trained the nervous system to
respond to life with 'allowing'
rather than 'Resistance'

It IS that simple. And your body will learn how to do it. It has already mastered countless other tasks and made them an everyday occurrence. It can and will do this too. But it requires training. Training and practice!

OK, let's apply the bike riding metaphor to 'allowing'. Where is this Allowing bike that I can get on and start riding? It is right here. It is so right here in fact, that you didn't even recognize it.

The bike is your body, or rather, your nervous system.

Chapter 8
Let's Take A Ride!

"If you worried about falling off the bike, you'd never get on." - Lance Armstrong

Let me lead you through the first and simplest of the 'allowing' exercises. This is not a thinking exercise. When you learned to ride a bike, you didn't have to think about it. You didn't study books and review videos. You just tried to do it and then, without you having to force it, your body learned to *feel* it.

The same approach is adopted here. You learn to feel what is actually going on, and then 'Allow' your body to master reacting to that in such a way that you will stay upright and balanced. The difference here is that with 'allowing' training', we are not responding to events from the environment outside of us. We are responding to events in the environment **inside** of us. In the beginning, we are not the least bit concerned about what is going on outside. Eventually yes, but in the beginning no.

In this training, you learn to actually feel your body and everything that is going on there, *and let it be there*. To ride the 'allowing' bike means:

> ***Giving yourself permission to feel
> whatever you are feeling, fully, without
> judgment or criticism, without any
> story about it, and without any
> intention to change it***

That is why it is so hard. We are NOT doing self-help here. We are NOT doing personal development. We are NOT trying to force ourselves into new behaviors. We are NOT trying to fix anything. We

76

have NO agenda other than to feel what is here, and let the body's own innate ability to respond take over.

It Knows What To Do

The human body is, without a doubt, the most complex, sophisticated, and intelligent object in the universe. Thirteen billion years in the making, it is the absolute pinnacle of creation. It is the most flexible and adaptable mechanism in existence. It has, built into it, the capacity to respond to absolutely any event that could possibly occur. And it can even do it with grace, style, and even flava!

In other words folks, *it knows what to do*. If you give it a chance to do it, yes you will find that it already knows.

> *"When the water comes out of the mountain, it doesn't need a GPS to find the ocean. It knows where to go." - Michael Brown*

Just like the body "knew" that it needed to keep you upright when you were learning to ride that bike, it also knows that it needs to keep you "upright" in every other aspect of your life.

I repeat: Your body already knows what to do

It responded to the environment when you were a child to protect you and make sure you got your needs met. It can just as easily, and just as automatically, respond to your current environment (including your now spiritually developed consciousness) to bring about the life you have always dreamed of having.

But first you have to make your environment safe for it, and then you have to let it do whatever it needs to do in order to make the transition. This willingness (and, dare I say, trust) is the heart and soul of the 'Tao Of Allowing'.

Shut Up & Listen

This all starts by simply listening to this remarkable organism; this remarkable, living machine that has been selflessly serving you since that one little sperm won the race and started this whole process in motion! 'Allowing' starts with simple body awareness.

You feel your body, just as it is. **Feel it!** Not think about it. Not analyze it. Not decide what it should be. Not judge whether it is a good or a bad feeling. For a brief period of time, you suspend judgment, resistance, criticism, distraction, avoidance, and you just feel what is there. You 'allow' whatever is there to be there, even if it is uncomfortable, in fact, *especially*, if it is uncomfortable.

So let me walk you through an exercise right now. It's very simple, and you will have to close your eyes for it, but, if you don't have the audio book version, then just memorize the instructions.

(By the way, you can get the audio book for free by visiting http://JustAllowIt.net/TaoOfAllowing.)

OK, now on with the exercise.

- Close your eyes

- Focus your attention on the way your body feels

- For the time being, just ignore the way your mind will describe what is going on (it always wants to comment, describe, and narrate)

- Just FEEL it (for you technical types, they call it the kinesthetic sense)

- Allow whatever is there to be there, even if you don't like it

- Notice what is there, and, for just a little bit of time, don't try to change it, fix it, adjust it or even want it to be anything other than what it is

- If you can do that even for 5 seconds you have experienced 5 seconds of 'allowing'

- And if you can't? We'll get to that in a minute!

That is it. That is all there is to it, but, before you try the exercise, let me provide a little heads-up on what to expect when you start doing it.

- Your attention WILL wander

- Your mind WILL speak up

- You WILL want to distract yourself

- You WILL wonder, "Am I doing this right?"

- You WILL think, "What is supposed to be happening?"

- You WILL resist (remember that has become your default state)

Just let all of those sensations, emotions, thoughts, memories, and associations come and go. You might even say to your mind "Thank you, but I don't need you right now!"

And, oh yeah, one more thing, **JUST FEEL IT**.

OK, now you try it! Take the plunge!

By the way, in addition to (or instead of) the whole audio book you can also download these instructions as a short audio to help guide you while your eyes are closed. It's on the same page http://JustAllowIt.net/TaoOfAllowing..

Congratulations! You have just experienced 'allowing'. Most people are able to feel just a fleeting moment of release, but you also undoubtedly experienced just how hard that was to do. The reason it is hard proves my point, actually. That is the state of resistance, which has become the dominant state. And it is that state of resistance, which constitutes your vibrational set point (as they like to say in Law of Attraction circles). It is that which has been keeping you from being, doing, and having, everything you want to be, do, and have.

Congratulations again. Your eyes have been opened wide.

"You have just taken your first step into a larger world" - Obi Wan Kenobi

Let's Take A Look Under The Hood

So what just happened? Let's take a closer look.

If you are like most people (and who isn't?) then you had a very hard time doing this. I mean, really, why is it that you couldn't just sit with what is going on inside of you without fidgeting, or being distracted, or wondering how long it's been?

That Is The State Of Resistance!

There it is, as plain as day. What you felt was the state of resistance that has become your normal state. Not your *natural* state, mind you, but unfortunately, the *normal* one.

> *If 'allowing' had been your natural state, this exercise would have been easy, even pleasurable!*

In that brief exercise, if you were even a little willing to just be with what was there, then you experienced the State of Allowing. If you weren't able to do it, then you certainly got a good look at what has become your normal state. Stick with me. This is only the first time you got on the bike. You fell over right away. No surprise there, but just stick with me, and you will eventually feel that moment of release.

Whether you felt even a moment of the State of Allowing or none at all, you have still accomplished the critical first step. You now know that your normal state is resistance. I know that the state of resistance is not what we want, but the first step in relieving it, is realizing that we are in it. Recognizing the symptoms of resistance, and just how deeply engrained it is within us, is the unavoidable (albeit unpleasant) first step.

The Shift Of Perception

What we call ah-ha moments, or, great insights, are shifts in perception. What we once saw one way, we now see a different way. Or, like what just happened, we become aware of something which, moments before, we were almost completely unaware of!

This shift is the lynchpin on which all spiritual growth occurs. Without it, nothing really changes. We need to see things differently. It is that shift of perception, that new vision that drives the nervous system to make the necessary changes that will eventually embody that vision into our normal behavior.

So recognizing resistance *as* resistance, qualifies for a major breakthrough. Believe me, even if nothing in your life has changed, you have turned a major corner.

Since recognizing resistance is the first step, let's take a moment and do that right now. Jot down on a piece of paper five things or people in your life that you consistently feel a sense of resistance about. Then write down what that resistance feels like in your body.

You don't have to do anything with this yet. Just become aware. Oh, and be honest. Sometimes we are resistant to the people that are closest to us.

Now, let's walk another block. There are some more corners waiting.

I Allowed...

"'Allowing' as taught by GP, has proven to be the doorway to what I had always been seeking. While I experienced great things with many techniques, there was always an underlying agenda to fix a "problem," preventing me from seeing beyond my current identity and moving into the truth. 'Allowing' has provided access to the deepest levels of peace and self-knowledge. This has led to concrete improvements in all areas of my life, from confidence, concentration, health and the ability to perform, to connecting better with others. The inner resource to finally know how to handle anything that arises is probably the greatest gift of all."

~ Evan

Chapter 9
The State Of Resistance

"To fight and conquer in all our battles is not supreme excellence; supreme excellence consists in breaking the enemy's resistance without fighting." - Sun Tzu

I know it is hard to hear, but, we are all in the state of resistance way more often than not. I am actually bold enough to assert that it is 95% of our reactive behavior. Unfortunately, resistance is the *dominant* state. In other words, resistance is our vibrational set point. Ouch!

Resistance is so engrained into our behavior (individual and collective), that we don't even realize it. So, while on a conscious level, we affirm all the good things we want, we meditate, we visualize, we keep our thoughts positive. At the very same time, the state of resistance is lying there dormant, just waiting for the environment to do something, at which point it will spring into action and push away the very thing we have been visualizing.

So, is there a way out of this state?

> **"Sometimes, the only way to win is not to play." - Joshua the computer in the movie War Games**

Mercifully, there is! And I am going to get to it straight away. For now, just accept that you are chronically in a state of resistance, even though you are not aware of it. Trust me on this. I will prove it to you in a minute.

The real reason you are not allowing all the goodies into your life, the real reason the Law of Attraction is not working as advertised, is because you are not actually in the State of Allowing. Moreover, all of the visualizations, positive thinking, inner game, goals, and accountability partners, or any other technique or process you may be using, will be *totally* impotent in the face of these pre-programmed states.

Totally?

Yep, *totally*.

Are you beginning to see why your attempts at the Law of Attraction have been a bit less than stellar?

Is That Me?

The state of resistance has become *so much* your state, that you probably say, "oh, that is just the way I am."

Wrong! It is NOT the way you are. It is the way you were **trained** to be. Yes, there is a really big difference. But now (drum roll) the good news:

> ***Anything trained into us***
> ***can be trained out of us,***
> ***and, new patterns, better***
> ***patterns, and natural***
> ***patterns, will emerge in***
> ***their place.***

So, since 'allowing' is not something you do, how do you learn it? Ready for another shocker? You don't! Nope, you do NOT learn it. You **train** it.

Stick with me. It gets easier.

Walk, Talk, Resist

'Allowing' is our natural state. We are all born that way. I know it doesn't feel that way now, but that is how we started. The very thing that makes human survival possible is, unfortunately, the very thing that also creates the biggest obstacle to a life of richness, creativity, and, prosperity.

The Learning Machine

As I touched on earlier, the human body is a miraculous machine. The adaptability of us humans is amazing. The fact that we live in pretty much every environment on earth is a testament to how well we adapt. Even when the environment is extremely harsh, the body finds a way to make it work. We are downright Gumbies, bending into any shape we need to in order to survive. But...

> *The very mechanism that allows us to walk, talk, even dance, without thinking about it, is the very same mechanism that installs resistance as our normal state*

Why does it do that? Because it can, and because it has to.

Even though we are born in a natural state of allowing, expectation, and enthusiasm, the need to survive will, and does, override all of that when it required to do so. We will bend ourselves completely out of our natural shape in order to survive our environment.

Sadly enough, we needed to do just that.

The way in which the nervous system accomplishes that bending is to shut down anything that does not directly relate to surviving, and create behaviors favorable to the authorities in the environment. In other words, it creates behavior that conforms to The Law of the Tribe.

Survival is the mandate of the nervous system... it trumps everything

When we are children, we are totally vulnerable, weak, and, powerless. We must be protected by our family, our tribe, our caregivers, or we do not survive. So when we meet with any kind of threat from those who are entrusted with and responsible for our care, it is interpreted by the nervous system as a life-threatening situation.

I do not mean the obvious examples of extreme abuse. I mean the everyday stuff of disapproval, guilt, shame, being ignored, diminished, made small, etc. Any time something we care about is belittled, berated, or goes unrecognized, we are threatened, and we learn the lesson. That behavior has to go. Even an unspoken undercurrent that you are not acceptable as you are, is enough to do the trick.

In the watershed book *"The Drama of the Gifted Child"*, Alice Miller recounts the story of picking up a young girl who had been fairly regularly abused and neglected. She put her in the car, shut the door, and then walked around to the driver's side and got in. She started the car and as she turned around to start backing out of the driveway, she noticed that the little girl's face was white as a ghost and she had this terribly pained expression. She asked her what was wrong but the little girl didn't answer. Then she noticed that the girl's fingers had gotten shut in the car door and were stuck there.

She ran around to her side of the car and opened the door, picked her and up and comforted her. There was no permanent damage to her fingers you will all be happy to know, but, the lesson of that story couldn't be more clear. This mechanism of controlling behavior is unmovable when it has to be. That little girl had been trained that is was less dangerous to endure horrible pain than to voice that pain and look for relief. That little girl's nervous system had set up an energetic assumption that it was more dangerous to cry out for help than to just experience the pain.

The power of suppression is formidable.

Thankfully, most of us did not have to experience anything that extreme. Our suppression didn't have to go to work on that level... or did it?

When we look back on childhood experience and see it through the eyes of an adult, we may be tempted to think, "oh that wasn't *that* big a deal." And it wasn't ... at least from an adult's point of view, but, to a child, whose entire world revolves around mom and dad and any other people of authority, it is a matter of utmost seriousness. It is a matter of life and death.

Any parental disapproval, however small, is interpreted by the little body's nervous system as a threat to survival

The penalty for breaking The Law of the Tribe is always the same, death. At least, to a totally powerless and dependent little one, that is what it feels like, and that is what the nervous system assumes.

So, whenever the child's little world is threatened, at that very moment, without any delay, the system kicks in to protect him or her. The fact is, they cannot protect themselves and the nervous system must do its job without any input from its owner. And so, it is automatic, irresistible and total and there is nothing you can do about it. The very environment, which is supposed to be safe and supporting, is instead creating distress and a feeling of being at risk of not surviving. So the survival mechanism kicks in and starts shutting things down, adjusting behavior, and guaranteeing that the little person remains safe. Or, at least, as safe as is possible. Survival is the mandate and it holds the ultimate trump card. It operates without the need for consent.

What does it shut down? Well, anything it needs to! That will include things we are really quite fond of, such as, happiness, individuality, creativity, openness, trust, expressiveness, confidence, curiosity, a sense of self-worth, value and expectancy of good and, of course, 'allowing'.

Yeah, not insignificant stuff.

So, instead of being naturally 'allowing' and expectant, we become guarded and closed. The degree of resistance will be in direct proportion to how much you were not loved or acknowledged. I don't mean acknowledge for "good" behavior, but acknowledged for just being you.

I hope it is clear now that, even though 'allowing' is natural to us, for all of us to some degree, it has been conditioned out of our systems by necessity. I do want to emphasize that. It was conditioned out of us **by necessity**. If it hadn't, none of us would have made it into kindergarten, let alone to adulthood.

As I have said time and time again, awareness is the first step towards healing. Think back right now and try to remember five incidents in which you were totally expressive, totally yourself, and you felt shut down. I know these things are a bit uncomfortable, maybe even painful to remember, but, believe me, this is the information you need to free yourself from unnecessary restrictions on your happiness.

Write down how you felt: same, guilt, confusion, anger, sadness, disappointment, discouragement. Try to feel what happened.

Choice? What Choice?

Choice is an adult idea. We love that idea and cling to it, defend it, and even fight for it. Having choice is the essence of our ideas of freedom and the good life. But how much choice do we really have?

You did not choose to be trained into the state of resistance. And as long as you are in it, you are not choosing any of the reactions to your environment. None! Ouch!

We start out life without choice. We end up in families that are not of our choosing and learn The Law of The Tribe by simply downloading it. We do not question the wisdom of our elders until we have already absorbed most, if not all, of their beliefs, attitudes, rules and points of view. Then, what's to question?

Since we were too young to choose, too undeveloped to understand, and too powerless to change the environment or get out of it, the nervous system, with its mandate to survive, and its power of suppression, took over in order to guarantee that we do, in fact, make it to adulthood.

And it worked! You did make it. You are here now reading this book because your system protected you when you couldn't protect yourself. This protection came at a great price, to be sure, but the system did what it was designed to do. It got you to here, to right now, to this time, when you *can* choose to make a change. You can choose to train the system in such a way that it not only survives, but *thrives*.

Chapter 10
Exploring The Resistant State

"If I have resistance to something, it means there's something wrong. The resistance to me is a sign of fear." - Billy Corgan

How do we undo that training and put some new and better training in its place? Or, even better, discover and liberate the natural, authentic behavior that got suppressed instead?

Like any new way of being, mastering 'allowing' requires both theory and practice. We really do need to understand what is happening so we can direct the process of retraining, and we must practice this training in the same way an athlete trains for a big game. With total focus, dedication and commitment.

"Practice 'allowing' the way an athlete trains for the big game"

So first, we must become really adept at recognizing the state of resistance when it is triggered. Remember, these programmed responses are **automatic**. They happen without any thought on your part. Just like lifting your hand up to scratch your nose requires no thought whatsoever. You just do it. Even so, the various patterns of resistance and defense happen totally without input from you. They are so automatic in fact, and have been around for so long, that you have actually begun to believe that *that is the way you are*!

Recognizing resistance AS resistance, and NOT you, is an essential component in the mastering of 'allowing'.

You have actually come to believe that those behaviors are you, rather than what they really are. And what are they really? Artificial behaviors, adapted and programmed into the nervous system so that you could **hide** who you really are from the environment and instead, display a totally fictitious character that fit the expectations of The Tribe. It was that for which you won approval and remained safe. Since it really was dangerous for you, that strategy was a very good one, and, I might add, very effective too.

But, these behaviors are **not** you. They never have been and they never will be. Who you really are lies on the other side of this manufactured behavior, and that is the real treasure we are after.

The system did its job. That is an incontestable fact. And, because it did its job, you are now a developed adult. That means that now, you *do* have the capacity, the discernment, and the will, to start the process of making different decisions, different choices, and thus *reclaim* the lost *State of Allowing*. This will establish a totally new, and increasingly more functional relationship with your environment, your life, your career, the whole enchilada. But, more importantly, it will re-establish your relationship with your soul.

We need to do this wisely however. Wisely and thoroughly, in fact. Simply recognizing that 'allowing' is the natural state, and that you do have access to it, is not enough. The nervous system is doing way too good a job at keeping it hidden. So, in addition to the simple practice of body awareness, which I introduced above, we also need some education and some more advanced exercises.

It IS All About You!

As I say all the time in my Law of Attraction 2.0 course:

"**To study the Law of Attraction, is to study** *yourself*"

To walk the "Tao Of Allowing" is to walk as yourself in harmony with the reality of all things. In order to do that and become a master at it, we must first become master students. We must become thoroughly aware of the way in which the state of resistance has been operating, and then master the means by which we disengage it.

So let's take a look at this state that we are in most of the time and, as you now know, you no longer need.

The Symptoms Of The Resistant State

At the risk of over-repeating myself, (I know. It's already too late!) resistant behaviors operate on autopilot. They have been functioning almost totally out of your conscious control, even out of your conscious awareness. So, obviously, the very first step is to become conscious of how they are operating.

'Resistance' is the polar opposite of 'allowing', and you are either in one or the other - there is no neutral ground.

'Resistance' and 'allowing' are mutually exclusive. You are either in one or the other. There is no neutral ground here, no DMZ. Don't get me wrong, it doesn't mean that you are either 100% 'resistant' or 100% 'allowing'. The nervous system is a very complex instrument. Layer upon layer of reactive behaviors have been created to respond to all of the things that happen regularly in your environment, and there are a lot of them.

Depending on what happens, you will react either from the 'resistant' or the 'allowing' state, but you will always react from one of those, and *only* one at a time. Those are the two camps, and I don't know of any others.

So what we are concerned with here is the dominant state. That is, which of those two states is most often triggered? When the environment throws something at us, which state is most likely to respond? For most of us, most of the time, it is the resistant state that gets the call. Resistance is the go-to player.

States Manifest As Reactions

We tend to think of resistance in terms of the behaviors that manifest it. Resistance is way more than a reaction, it is in itself a state of the nervous system. All of the various symptoms of resistance are actually *manifestations* of the resistant state.

Resistance is not an attitude, a thought, or an emotion. However, it does *manifest* itself as any and all of those. Resistance is a state, and, as a state, it is simply the way the system will react to a given event in the environment, when the event occurs. So, when not triggered, resistance is not felt. It is only experienced when something in the environment triggers it.

That leads to a rather startling conclusion.

> ***You can be in a***
> ***predominantly resistant***
> ***state even when you don't***
> ***feel it***

In more advanced exercises, I would have you imagine things to purposely trigger the resistant reactions. That is actually necessary since we don't know we are in that state unless we get triggered.

Vibrational set point is a term that has gotten coined by the Law of Attraction community. I hope you can see now that being in this state of resistance, even though it is not felt, *is* your vibrational set point. That is what keeps us from living in the natural and magical *State of Allowing*. It keeps us off the path, out of the Tao, as it were. No wonder we aren't manifesting at the level we want to.

So let's start looking at how resistance is reflected in our lives. All of the symptoms that I am going to mention in the several pages that follow, can be classified as *'expressions'*, or, *'manifestations'* of the resistant state. This state is experienced in all three of the following modes:

- Physical Sensation

- Emotion

- Thought

Let's look at them each individually.

Physical Sensation

When the resistant state is triggered, we feel it as physical tension. It is a feeling of defensiveness or self-protection. Quite appropriate because that is exactly what it is. The body is ready to defend itself. It doesn't matter if the threat is real or imaginary, by the way.

It will usually come with some kind of a feeling of physical tightness associated with it and it is also usually localized. That is, it will tend to be felt in specific areas of your body. There are three places in the body that it is most commonly felt:

- The solar plexus (a.k.a. the gut)

- The chest

- The top of the torso

Most people have their "favorite" place. In fact, the place in your body where you most often feel it can be a key in identifying the nature of the original circumstances or traumas that put the programming into place.

I will not get into an in depth analysis in this book (it is a study in itself). If you want to delve into this aspect on a much deeper level, I would strongly suggest you read my book *"The 7 Eyes of the Soul."*

Briefly, here is a rough guideline of the most likely meaning:

Physical Sensation - The Solar Plexus (a.k.a. the Gut)

Tension or pressure in the solar plexus usually means that your ability to own your desires (maybe even admit that you had them) and have them met was shut down by moral judgment or shame. The natural expression of who you are was not allowed because it wasn't "right" behavior. It really didn't matter that it was your natural behavior. It was regarded as wrong, perhaps even sinful. This is not the same, by the way, as being taught what is appropriate or inappropriate. It was not the behavior that was bad. It was you.

This is the territory of guilt and shame. It is simply not safe to be yourself, or to own your own desires and interests, and exercise the power to get those needs met. So circumstances in your life that require you to shine, to take the lead, or merely honestly ask for what you want, will trigger the resistant state. The nervous system has put in place an energetic assumption that it isn't safe to even ask for what you want, let alone get it. That kind of triggering will most likely be felt right in the gut.

Equally noteworthy is the fact that it doesn't matter whether you want the thing, or don't want the thing!. They are both the same to the nervous system. So whether you are being given a promotion or being fired is of no importance. The reaction of resistance remains the same. It is not the thing itself, so much that it is triggering the system. It is the call to step up, assume a higher degree of personal power, and honestly admit to what you desire. That is against the rules and so cannot be allowed expression.

Physical Sensation - The Chest

Tension or pressure in the chest usually means that your natural desire to connect to others, to trust, to be curious, and even to love was restricted. You were taught to mistrust, maybe even reject, those who were not like your tribe. (That includes you by the way.)

The natural curiosity and willingness to love, to accept others (and ourselves), and to allow things into our lives, was replaced by a closing down of the heart in a self-protecting, and isolating, inner gesture. It is fascinating to see that the tension in the chest often feels like a building up of pressure from the inside. It feels like something trying to get out. There *is* something trying to get out. You are. That is, your natural affections, love and willingness and desire to connect.

Again, notice that even if you really want to express more affection and love or curiosity, the system has been programmed to assume that such behavior is dangerous. The energetic assumption is that, "connecting is not safe" (unless they are just like The Tribe and often not even then). Assume the defensive posture, and right on cue, there will be the tension in the chest. It is the system's attempt to protect the sensitive area.

Physical Sensation - The Top Of The Torso

The top of the torso includes the jaw, the neck and the shoulders. Tension or pressure in this area is most often caused by having had your natural self-expression squashed. This could have been

104

accomplished by criticism and judgment, by being told that you weren't good enough, maybe even being treated like you were a disappointment, even if it was never actually said. You needed to just be like everybody else. Don't stand out, unless, of course, it was as a model of conformity.

It could also have been the result of being diminished or belittled, even ignored. That picture you drew, to which your Dad said, "keep trying kid" and you could just feel the disinterest. Maybe you were asked why you couldn't be more like that perfect kid down the street who is always covered in gold stars.

Absolutely No Absolutes Folks... Really... No Kidding

These are, of course, just basic guidelines. These definitions are not absolute (*nothing is*) and your symptoms may vary. The best way to discover the source of some tension in the body is to practice 'allowing'. The tension itself will eventually reveal to you its story.

> *The best way to find out where
> the tension is coming from, is to
> ask it!*

It gets pretty obvious that, if you are going to ask it directly what its story is, then you are going to have to allow it to be there first.

Resistance can be felt anywhere, of course. I, myself, often feel it as a kind of unpleasant tingling all over my skin, like an electric current looking for a light bulb to light up. The solar plexus, the chest, and the shoulder and jaw seem to be focal points for most people.

It is no accident that these areas correspond to energy centers known as Chakras. (Again, more on that in my other book "The 7 Eyes of the Soul.")

Emotion

We also experience resistance as emotions, like the feeling of anxiety (fear without an obvious cause), and, in extreme cases, dread. Resistance does, in fact, trigger the entire range of emotions that we humans are capable of. It can be a subtle feeling of waiting for the other shoe to drop, or feeling unprepared. It can also appear as restlessness, dissatisfaction, and worry, as well as self-doubt, second-guessing, procrastinating, avoiding, irritability, sensitivity. It is a very long list.

The point here is to not catalogue all the possible ways in which it can appear, as much as it is to see clearly that they all have a single source, namely, your resistant state. Then, you learn to read your own energetic signature and discern your favorite flavor.

According to research, there aren't that many emotions to be had. Of course, they can combine and recombine to make a virtually unlimited amount of experiences, but, it all breaks down to six:

- Love/Desire

- Joy/Happiness

- Surprise/ Amazement

- Anger/Rage

- Sadness/Grief

- Fear/Anxiety

These constitute the palette of emotions that can, and do, get generated by interaction with the environment. There is no need to go into each of these in detail, but, suffice it to say that one of these is way more prevalent and powerful than the rest.

Guess which one?

It's a no-brainer actually. Fear.

And why fear? As I mentioned earlier, the number one mandate of the whole system is survival. If that is threatened (real or imagined), the response we now know as fear kicks in to get us out of there. Fear is the body's natural reaction to a threat.

Now here is the rub. The nervous system has been programmed so that, expressing who you really are, is regarded as a threat, or that it will at least lead to one very shortly. That means that the heightened state of alertness that we know of as fear, is the number one tool in the toolbox of resistance.

Let me repeat that in bold letters:

The nervous system has been programmed so that expressing who you really are is regarded as a threat.

And I might also point out, a threat that it is perfectly defended against. Fear is what gives resistance its authority, and is why it feels so real and irresistible... even though it is actually neither! Fear triggers the entire survival mechanism making the suppression of your natural self a life threatening situation. The ultimate trump card.

This inevitably leads to an almost constant background noise of, "things are not OK as they are." Again, it does not matter whether the threat is real or imaginary. In fact, most of the time the threat is imaginary, but, as far as the resistant state is concerned, it is very real and requires immediate action. By the way, the state of resistance is the root of the pervasive modern disease, stress.

It should come as no surprise then that the resistant state, since it is in the act of withdrawing or avoiding is going to favor the three defensive emotions: anger, grief, fear, over the expressive ones: love, joy and amazement. It should be equally apparent that the resistant state is not open to being, having, and doing, all the things you want to have, be and do. Its agenda is not the same as yours and, when push comes to shove, the system wins every time.

Thought

Since we are living in this state of resistance pretty much all the time, our thought patterns have developed over time to explain and interpret our experience.

Feeling always comes first. Thought is an explanation and interpretation, after the fact. It is never the source!

The feelings (emotions and physical sensation) came first. Thoughts came later. Much later. Most of this state of resistance was put into place before we could even speak, let alone think. Later, when our minds began to develop and we needed to have explanations as to why we were the way we were, concepts, ideas, associations, interpretations and stories, emerged. In other words, thought.

Of course, our parents, teachers, schools, religions, and the entire culture were there, ready to provide you with all the reasons why the resistant state was the *right* one. No need to doubt or even question.

Skepticism, cynicism, distrust, suspicion, expectation of the worst, risk aversion, playing it safe, philosophies of caution, defensive posturing, conservatism, conformity, and valuing the group over the individual, all arise from the state of resistance.

Resistance to change, fundamentalism, dogmatism, and strict adherence to ideologies, are all symptoms of the resistant state. Thinking that the world is a dangerous place, that people are out to get us, and that defending ourselves is a duty, are all the noble disguises that resistance wears when it appears as thought and belief systems.

Unless we get trained otherwise, our thoughts do nothing other than explain and justify why resistance is the only reasonable position to take. We are, of course, questioning that right now in this book. So even though thoughts came later, they are very powerful and, in fact, are the first place where the reality of our experience begins to shine through.

Once you get thoroughly convinced that the resistant state is not the best state to be in, we can then begin the process of retraining. It is not easy, but once convinced that this is the way to go, you then muster the faith and commitment to get back on that bike again and again.

This is why Law of Attraction teachers focus so much on the mental aspect of it, but that is also why it is not effective on its own. The mental game is important only so far as it keeps you working on the inner game, the emotional game. To know you are in the resistant state empowers you to enter fully into the process of retraining and eventually gain your freedom.

So thoughts are equally powerful for good or for ill. Also fascinating to note is that thoughts are far more tenacious than feelings. They can inspire you with the vision that will help you persist but they are equally capable of shutting down the entire process of 'allowing'. This is why, in those beginning exercises, we simply don't pay attention to thoughts. We simply say, "thanks, but I don't need you now." The habit of constantly judging, describing, and narrating every experience is deeply engrained in us, and is the number one distraction from a consistent and deepening practice of the 'Tao Of Allowing'.

A Quick Word About Beliefs

When I use the word belief, I am not talking simply about a mental position or opinion. I am not even talking about the emotional attachment to that position or opinion. I am talking about the entire makeup of the nervous system. The "beliefs" (actually the **laws**) of your tribe of origin were installed as programs. It was those laws that formed the concepts that we later named beliefs. Beliefs and states you can actually think of as synonymous.

I also used the term *energetic assumptions*, and by that, I mean the same thing as beliefs, but on a much deeper level. I think that term is more accurate because it involves the whole system: body, mind, emotions, and soul. Beliefs are way more than the thoughts you have. Thoughts are merely one form of expression that a belief takes.

It does go the other way as well. We continue to form energetic assumptions in adulthood. It doesn't end with childhood. It's just that because children don't have any defenses, and are always living in the State of Allowing, that the beliefs sink in quickly and without resistance. Add to that, as children, we are genuinely powerless, dependent, and with almost no control over our environment. You can see why the majority of these "beliefs" are installed during this time. The majority to be sure, but not the only ones.

Thoughts will congeal into beliefs. Once you decide something is true, the thought moves from being just a thought to being an assumption. That is exactly what happened as a child, but the decision was not a conscious one. It was pure survival mechanism. Good thing for that really, since none of us would have survived otherwise.

Assumptions

Assumptions are something accepted just as they are. They are not *proven truth*, but rather *believed truth*. They don't get questioned, until of course, the results you are getting in your life suck so bad that you start looking for the cause. (Suffering is a great fan of consciousness.) When suffering occurs, the assumptions get called up and questions start being asked. 'Bout time!

But, even though thoughts congeal into beliefs later in life, they will almost always be governed by the earlier patterns put into place. There is a much larger context, namely energetic assumptions, that is determining the form thoughts will take, but, take heart. The good news is, when it gets to fundamental beliefs, the most primary ones, there are not that many.

In fact, there is only one but that is the subject for another book. It's called "The Simple Truth." If you are interested.

So, remaining vigilant about what goes into your thinking as "truth", is still a necessary practice. It is way easier to reject a falsity before it gets in, rather than after. As you may have gleaned from what we have been talking about here, once a belief gets into the system, it is implemented as an automatic response, and, therefore, becomes invisible to our normal range of perception. It has become a state.

Are You Getting The Picture?

With all this going on, I think it becomes pretty apparent, why it is almost impossible to truly embrace something new coming into your life, unless of course, it is totally familiar and looks pretty much like what you expected it to... and sometimes not even then!

The state of resistance is constantly on the lookout for anything that does not fit within its rather narrow parameters of acceptability. But, isn't having new things come into our lives exactly what we are actually seeking? Isn't that why we embarked on this whole personal development path in the first place? Isn't that why you watched "The Secret" two hundred times? C'mon. Admit it!

Can you see now why, when you thought you were practicing 'allowing' you were, in fact, thoroughly engaged in resistance?

Don't think that because we are focused on resistance that we are inviting negativity. It is only what we mistake as true, or identify with as yourself, that can harm you.

To see resistance as resistance,
and not as you, is to become
liberated from it

I am not emphasizing the negative. I am exposing the negative **as** negative. In order to do that, we must be willing to look at all the forms that the resistant state takes, and recognize them as resistance. Press on, amigos!

Chapter 11
The 9 Major Symptoms

"A well-trained mind responded to symptoms.
An ordinary mind reacted after it happened."
- Toba Beta

The state of resistance is the generic term for all of the symptoms of resistance. By now, you have probably recognized (albeit reluctantly) that you are feeling resistant most, if not all, of the time. Now let's look at some of the more specific ways in which this state manifests in our lives.

You will notice that, all of these symptoms appear as physical sensation, emotion, and thought. They pretty much always arise together. It is a system, after all.

As you are reading these, let yourself *feel* your reaction to them. This is not an intellectual exercise. Just filling up your mind with more information isn't going to heal or release anything. In fact, it often gets in the way. Look for that feeling of recognition in your body and the level of the intensity of that recognition.

1. "I am NOT safe": Lack of Protection or Insecurity

"If I allow things to be as they are, my life will go to hell in a hand basket." This is the mantra of resistance. This is a belief we all have that operates pretty much unseen. We believe that protection is not natural, that it is not my due as a human being; that I really am unsafe and I need to do whatever I can to make myself safe.

Safe! Safe! Safe! That is its only interest and concern. Happiness? Not important. Prosperity? Whatever! Self-expression? What's that?

We form a belief that, since it is not innate, safety must be acquired (sometimes by extreme measures) and that we haven't acquired it yet. So I can't walk the 'Tao Of Allowing'. If I do, I will get hurt, if not killed. If I don't 'Allow' it, I won't get hurt. To this belief, resistance seems the proper, even the natural, response and 'allowing' is not only "woo woo," it is stupid and naïve.

2. I have To DO Something

We are convinced that we have to DO something, anything, otherwise things will not go in a direction we like. We have to make them go the way we wish them to. But, the only thing this does is make struggle the characterizing quality of our lives.

> *Believe me, it is*
> *impossible to allow, or*
> *even enjoy, when you*
> *are struggling.*

And what if you really **don't** know what to do? Feeling like you must do something, and not knowing what, triggers the resistance big time. It makes us impulsive, reactive, unstable and fills the body with stress.

Stress = Resistance

119

In our culture, deciding to wait, postpone, or do nothing, is regarded as not being a decision at all. If there is anything I want to make clear to anyone who reads this book, is that struggle has become a way of life, and, friends, this should not be so!

Mind you, there are times when you must act and do so immediately, like when you step in front of an oncoming bus, but, for the most part, the feeling that you have to do something is an illusion, just part of the triggering of the resistant state.

3. I Won't Like What I Get

All of us are terrified that if we really do let go and **'Allow'**, what does come to us will be disappointing and may even be worse than what we already have.

Notice that, at the heart of this, there is almost no trust in the benevolence or the goodness of the universe. Nor is there any faith in our own capacity to create good things. Stop a minute and consider this. Don't just rush off to the next sentence. It'll wait.

Oftentimes, when we really become open to an answer to our needs or desires, the answer that comes doesn't always resemble what we had in mind. I know there are lots of stories of people doing their vision board or their visualization, and the thing appears in their life and looks exactly like they envisioned it. But the fact is, very often (more often, in fact) the first appearance doesn't look anything like the thing we visualized at all. Learning to trust in the benevolence of the universe allows you to patiently let things develop. The caterpillar comes first, then the butterfly. Always!

"The caterpillar comes first, then the butterfly. Always!"

4. I'll Believe It When I See It

Resistance is not only the opposite of 'allowing'; it is the opposite of *faith*. Faith is our capacity to expect good, even when we don't see any. It is our willingness to trust, to surrender, to feel like we are being taken care of and that life is basically good. You don't adopt a defensive posture against a benevolent force. Do you?

Resistance, on the other hand, assumes the worst, and won't change its mind until the perfectly good thing arrives. Of course, all the teachings of the Law of Attraction, as well as religious faith, declare exactly the opposite. You see it when you believe it.

It is taught that way because it is our inner vibration (our dominant state) that determines the outward experience. That is why I regard the Law of Attraction as a spiritual law and not simply a mental phenomena.

The Law of Attraction is a Spiritual Law

Since it is our inner energy that determines the outward experience then cultivating faith, hope, trust, and a feeling of worthiness and deserving is the obvious practice.

5. I Won't Like Who I Am

This belief, and the fear of putting it to the test (by actually discovering who you are), is probably the biggest symptom of all, and therefore, the block to everything. This is the one that gives resistance so much authority.

As I explained before, several times before in fact, when you were young and were threatened by something in your environment, the nervous system kicked in to protect you, because you were not ready to do that for yourself. I also explained that the system did that by shutting down whatever it needed to, including the very best parts of you.

What it shut down was specific, important aspects of yourself. It quite literally took parts of your real nature, innate character, and individuality, and made them inaccessible to you.

> *The nervous system literally cut off parts of yourself in order to protect what was left - and so, you became someone else*

What that did was create an image in your mind, that those parts of you that had to be cut off were not good. That was a totally reasonable and acceptable assumption, considering that, when you expressed them, you met with disapproval, rejection, and maybe even punishment or abuse. So now, as we start back into that territory, we are still laboring under the notion that **those parts of us are bad**. On an unconscious level, (the level of programmed response or energetic assumption), we are convinced that we can't allow ourselves to be ourselves.

Being "me" is dangerous. Ouch!

There lies, deeply within all of us, an almost silent belief that we really are bad, worthless, totally lacking in value, in beauty, totally unlovable, and needing to be contained and controlled - even deserving of punishment. Well, *excuse* me for living! The religious justification of that is what is called original sin. I cover that subject in depth in my book, "Original Innocence".

No wonder we are reluctant and resistant to let all those parts of us out. No wonder we are afraid of who we might actually be.

By the way, it doesn't matter how many people, with however much authority, tell you that you will discover that you are lovable, worthy and deserving, the resistant state is convinced that we are not. In fact, the resistant state cannot survive in the environment of genuine self-acceptance.

It will take faith to even begin to put this to the test. Yes, underneath all this programming, you are, and always have been, glorious beyond your imagination, but, your nervous system, programmed in the resistant state, **doesn't know that**. It is still living according to its energetic assumptions.

6. Attachment To A Particular Outcome

There is, within each and every one of us, a small part that **is** willing to allow good things into our lives. However, there is also a part of us that has really strict rules as to what the new thing needs to look like. Everything that does not look almost exactly the way we expect it to, gets rejected. This makes us anxious and frustrated and causes us to consistently let opportunity pass us by because we don't give it a chance to develop.

Reject all the caterpillars and you will never know a butterfly. Reject the acorn and you will never have an oak tree. Remember that the most beautiful building starts as a big pile of dirt and a big hole in the ground, and that some of the most amazing substances make a really big, smelly, toxic mess when they are being created.

Almost nothing looks like the answer to your prayer when it first appears. After all, if you knew what you were looking for, you would have found it and brought it into your life. But, you don't! That means, you have no idea what the real answer to your prayer will look like. It may look like an angel. But it may, just as easily, look like the belly of a whale. Burp!

7. Cultural Bias

Since you have read my explanation of resistance, and how it manifests in our thoughts and belief systems, it should not come as any great surprise that our entire culture is totally immersed in resistance as a way of life. Moreover, feeding our aversions, our distractions and our chronic avoidance is really big business.

The idea of happiness and peace welling up from within us, or being our natural state, is relegated to a fringe group of New Age wing nuts or spiritual people wearing funny clothes and sitting in really painful positions. Indeed, according to the mainstream, conventional wisdom, life is struggle and we should not only prepare for the worst, but also avoid feeling at all costs.

The messages of resistance, avoidance, denial, and defense, are everywhere. Is it any wonder why we don't even question these uncomfortable feelings, and so, live in an almost constant state of stress and insecurity?

Resistance IS our culture. Defense IS our culture.

Our culture is constantly bombarding us with messages, which, if not directly telling us to be frightened, (a.k.a. resistant) instead clearly implies it. All commercial messages have the following subtext planted firmly in the pretty words:

- You are not enough as you are (beautiful, thin, rich, strong, successful, smart, the list goes on and on)

- You should be afraid (of the past, present, and future)

- You do not have the resources for making it within yourself (you need my stuff)

None of those are true. None of them! But the fact that they are so pervasive makes it difficult to resist the popular currents. Not only that, but it adds a certain authority to the message. If you hear something often enough, you begin to accept it as true. I mean, everybody thinks that way, right? It becomes the conventional wisdom even if it is totally bogus, and, believe me, it is totally bogus!

8. Isolation or What About Me?

Everybody seems to be doing just fine, don't they? Everyone gets this Law of Attraction stuff, right?

Everyone is getting all the goodies, all the time. Everyone is manifesting the life of their dreams.

Everyone... except me!

Once you begin to become aware that you actually can have all the goodies but that you are not getting them, you think that you are the only one who feels this way.

This is made even more painful when you read all those glowing testimonials on the Law of Attraction guru web sites, and on those long form sales letters. There are all these hopelessly optimistic testimonials about all the people getting all these incredible manifestations just effortlessly pouring into their lives (right after they shelled out several hundred dollars for the home study course).

So, true to your resistant programming, you pull out your favorite stick and begin the process of beating yourself up because all that hasn't happened for you. And it is clearly your fault. It works for everybody EXCEPT you! "What is the matter with me?"

In a word...nothing!

Those testimonials are the exceptions not the rule. Almost everybody is experiencing exactly what you are. And they all feel that they are the ONLY one who isn't getting the goodies. That is part of the insidious nature of resistance. It makes you feel totally alone and isolated. And then, to add a drop of gall to the soup, it makes you feel ashamed for feeling that.

The facts never change the state. Even though it may feel as though you are the only one, you have to remember that this is part of the programming of resistance. You most certainly are not the only one, not by a long shot. As a matter of fact, you are the majority! Almost everyone feels that way. You couldn't feel otherwise. Unless, of course, your particular Tribe taught you total self-acceptance.

Could I get a show of hands of those people who were raised with total self-acceptance?

9. Fear Of Loss

We are so afraid that if we really do 'allow', if we really do open our hands to receive more, then what we already have will fall out of them, never to be retrieved.

Yes, you do have to release your grip on what you have in order to have an open hand to receive more. You have to be willing to let go of the things that are no longer serving you, in order to have room to welcome in what will. Most of us even recognize that that is so.

Nonetheless, we deeply fear losing what we already have. We are very reluctant to let go of what we have *before* we see something better. We do this even if what we have is really small, insignificant, and inadequate, or, if we simply don't like what we have. *"Better the devil you know than the devil you don't know"* as the old adage goes.

There is probably nothing more difficult than to let go of something before you have a replacement. That is why the breakup of a relationship, or the loss of a job, is so devastating. We go from having something, even an inadequate something, to having nothing, and we fear that we will never again have anything ever again.

The fact that the fear is groundless and is untrue, doesn't matter to the state of resistance. For it, permanent loss is a real possibility and it does not want to take the chance. Fact is, permanent loss is no more a real possibility than permanent gain. Impermanence is the nature of life.

Permanent loss is no more a real possibility than permanent gain.

The willingness to let things go with equanimity is one of the biggest blessings of the 'Tao Of Allowing'. It fills life with an unspeakable sweetness and lights us up with a vision that recognizes the unique value of everything. The impermanence that fills us with so much worry is the very thing that makes everything so precious.

All My Symptoms

I hope you have recognized these symptoms in yourself. The point of this book is not a mere intellectual inquiry, but a deep and experiential one. This isn't really a book. It is your life.

To *recognize* the symptoms of the dominant state, is the very first step at *changing* that state, or, perhaps more accurately, leaving behind the unnatural and acquired state of resistance and rediscovering your natural and stress free state of 'allowing'.

So take a moment right now and choose your top three favorite forms of resistance. Yes I know it won't be fun, but, don't forget that the first step, as always, is awareness. Now take your top three and notice where you feel it most. Is it emotional? Which emotions does it evoke. Is it psychological? What thoughts, images or memories appear? Is it physical? What part of the body does it most effect?

Again write this down. It helps it sink in.

Chapter 12
5% For ... 95% Against

"I watched what method Nature might take, with intention of subduing the symptom by treading in her footsteps." - Thomas Sydenham

According to the Law of Attraction teachings, it is the *dominant energy*, the dominant thoughts and feelings that get manifested in (and as) your life. This is the sum and substance of the whole vibrational match conversation that we hear all the time. "Be a vibrational match to what you're reaching for," asserts Abraham Hicks. This is true... but not quite. Some Law of Attraction teachers insist that it is the tenor of your thoughts, that make up your vibrational set point. Others, like Abraham Hicks insist that it is the emotions that are the key vibration that invokes the Law of Attraction.

Thoughts and emotions are to vibration what sneezing and coughing are to a cold - the symptoms, not the cause

As we have already seen, both thoughts and emotions are the manifestation of something much more fundamental, so simply trying to change either the emotional or mental states (or physical, for that matter) without first releasing the underlying state is a bit like trying to grow a tree by throwing leaves in the air. It may be pretty for a minute, but the wind will blow them away shortly.

States, not emotions or thoughts, ARE your vibrational set point

This is a big one to get. We usually think of vibration as the way we are feeling, or the feeling we get from someone else. "They have a really nice vibe," we would say. It is even taught that way. But, it isn't so. Your vibrational set point is the way you **will** feel when some event happens in your life. In other words:

The state you are predominantly in is your vibrational set point. And it doesn't matter whether you are feeling it now or not.

Think of the string of a guitar. The E string on a guitar will always sound an E when it is plucked. When it is plucked you hear the E as a vibration. But the vibrational set point of a guitar string is not the sound it makes. It is the sound it inevitably will make. Of course, that is assuming that the guitar is in tune. Tuning is, after all, what this book and all of 'allowing' is about.

Since the vast majority of us live in a habitual state of resistance, is it any wonder that we have not actually experienced the great promise that personal development and the Law of Attraction hold out? Obviously, changing that state is the name of the game, and not, trying to generate new emotions. Tuning the guitar is the mission; not trying to change the sound once is has sounded. Ever tried to catch a sound? That's right! Impossible.

Without a fundamental change or tuning to the underlying state, you will not be able to make any self-help technique work.

It would be like cleaning the sidewalk with a leaf blower. Yeah, it's clear here, but the debris is still around. It hasn't been removed. It has just been pushed out of site, perhaps over to your neighbor's lawn, who, in turn, will later be out with his leaf blower returning all the debris back to you!

The thing that people miss, and, frankly, is not often taught, is that we are not aware of the bulk of what is dominating our energy. Obviously, if the only time we are aware of our vibrational set point is **after** it has been triggered, and the behavior is already in play, then there is nothing to notice when it *isn't* being triggered. Like a guitar that has not been strummed.

We have all experienced this, right? You are feeling really good. Maybe you had something great happen for you, or, you just got out of a yoga class or a meditation session, and you are so peaceful and centered. Then someone cuts you off on the street, and you go off like a rocket. "WTF? Where did **that** come from?" you wonder. Just because you are not feeling it in the moment doesn't mean the state is gone. The guitar just got strummed... and it wasn't in tune.

So all of the techniques we do, visualization, positive thinking, vision boards, treasure maps, journaling, and any others you can think of, only reach so far. They are leaf blowers. Because, while the conscious 5% of you is totally in favor of being, doing, and having all the goodies, the other 95% of you is dead set against it.

Put This To the Test

It is really easy to put this to the test. In the beginning exercise, you were invited to just feel your body. Just feel it, nothing more. Just let yourself experience it as it is. Now, I want you to do the same thing, but this time picture something you really want but don't have. Picture something that really invokes the feeling of lack.

Now, rather than trying to force the feelings away and focus on the visualization or the desired result or whatever, instead, focus all your attention on the feelings that come up in response to the lack.

Same rules as before. Don't edit, judge, create a story or try to get rid of them. Actually allow them to happen. Just allow it. Observe them. If you are really ambitious, you can even try to move closer to them. We *want* to feel them. We *want* to observe the triggering. We want to find out if the guitar is in tune, and, if not (which is usually the case) how badly out of tune is it.

Watch what happens. Before starting the exercise however, consider one more thing.

Negative Emotions Are NOT Negative

You see, trying to hold the picture of what you want and get rid of all the "negative" feelings is extremely difficult. In fact, it is impossible. The only way we are able to get rid of them is to suppress the feelings, which doesn't get rid of them at all, of course. It just suppresses them and do remember...

It was the suppression of natural feelings that caused all this bad programming in the first place.

Once an emotion became unacceptable, we made up the story that the emotional response was "negative." It isn't. In fact, it may be extremely positive, but it is now being interpreted as "bad" as part of the strategy that keeps it suppressed. There are no such things as negative emotions. There are only natural emotions that got really bad press.

Obviously, we don't need more of the same. So, instead, let's do something really radical. Let's honor the system. Let's just sit here and watch the nervous system, in its state of resistance, and let it react. And always remember, that the only thing it is trying to do is keep you safe. That is its number one mandate. If it has been programmed to "believe" that there is something about what you are visualizing that could cause you harm, it will do its job and try to protect you from the imagined threat. It is going to resist it. Even if, on a conscious level, it could be the very best thing for you.

So, as you are feeling the resistance, just know that you have been triggered. The job then is not to make those "negative" feelings go away, but to show the nervous system that it is safe to both want and have what it is you are visualizing. I repeat:

The real goal is not to get rid of "negative" feelings but rather to convince the nervous system that it is safe

I know this is quite counterintuitive and completely contradicts the positive thinking school of conventional wisdom, but consider the following: The state that produces the negative thoughts and feelings is there. Does it really help to try to deny its existence? Isn't it a much more intelligent, not to mention compassionate, approach to actually turn toward the distress? To ask the resistant energy, "Who are you? What do you need? How can I help you?"

Imagine what your life would have been like if that is how you had been treated in the beginning.

OK, here is the revised exercise.

- Close your eyes

- Like before, focus your attention on the way your body feels

- Like before, just ignore the way your mind will describe what is going on (blah, blah, blah, it's all story)

- Just FEEL it

- Allow whatever is there to be there

- Now picture in your mind the thing you really want, but don't have

- Put all of your attention there and do your best to hold that picture

- Now consciously invite your nervous system to react to it

- If you are having a hard time even holding the picture, guess what? That is the nervous system resisting.

- Notice how you really want to get rid of all those feelings. That is also the resistant state

- Now just stay with it giving it full permission to react

- If you want you can even ask it;

- "Why is this dangerous?"

- "What is it about this that you don't like?"

- "What are you afraid of?"

- Just hold to it as long as you can

OK, now you try it.

I have this exercise recorded for you as well, so, if you would like it in audio form, you will find it on the same page as the others: http://JustAllowIt.net/TaoOfAllowing..

You may have experienced a great deal of resistance. Absolutely everyone does in the beginning, but just being willing to be with the system as it reacts and give it permission to do so, is the kindest thing you could ever possibly do for yourself.

In that moment, you are not suppressing, you are allowing. You are accepting. You have just become your body's friend. You have just taken the first step towards, not only becoming safe, but also becoming the master of your inner world.

This is the magic, and it is the real goal of the 'Tao Of Allowing'. Once the nervous system knows that it is safe, resistance is dropped. Boom! Gone! It has no interest in carrying it around once it is satisfied that it is no longer needed. It didn't take on the resistant state because it wanted to, or, because it thought it would be cool. It did it because it *had* to, and it will continue in that state for as long as it is convinced that it is necessary.

The body is not only incredibly loyal and persistent, it is also really smart. It doesn't hang on to anything it doesn't need, for even a second longer than is necessary.

You have just made resistance a little less-necessary.

There Is No Unconscious "Mind"

I know I have used the term unconscious. I have said things like we are unaware of these programs. But please don't go running off into that "unconscious mind" talk. When someone speaks of the "unconscious mind" they are actually referring to these states or programs.

What we call the "unconscious mind" is not a mind at all. It doesn't think, deliberate, plan, plot, or create. It doesn't hide in the bushes, waiting for you to walk by so that it can jump on you, seize your conscious mind, and mess up your life.

Calling it a mind has caused us to create all sorts of stories about it, and those stories have made it a bigger deal than it actually is.

What we call the unconscious mind is simply the dominant state of the nervous system.

That's it. Nothing more.

If you want to hear more of this you can check out my free video entitled "There Is No Unconscious Mind." It too is located at http://JustAllowIt.net/TaoOfAllowing.

Intentional Triggering

In the full audio/video training course "Just Allow It", I have people consciously picture things they both want and **don't want**. As a matter of fact, the third section in the course is entitled "Intentional Triggering" and I dedicated about an hour and a half to exploring different ways to get the energetic assumptions to react.

This is also a common practice in EFT (the Emotional Freedom Technique) which is a modality that I often use. I know it runs contrary to the positive thinking crowd, but the fact is, all of the positive thinking in the world will not reprogram a state. Thinking it will is a bit like jousting with windmills. For those of you who are not familiar with that metaphor I will put it in plain English. It's nuts!

So instead of trying to deny the so-called negative emotions or thoughts, I have people purposely trigger them by actively visualizing both the things they are attached to, and the things they are averse to. I want people to feel their deepest desires and their biggest fears, (which are actually two sides to the same coin.)

Using active imagination or visualization to draw pictures that the nervous system can react to, allows the person being trained in 'allowing', to discern the state of resistance (i.e. to see how well the guitar is tuned), own it, give it total permission to be there, and thus show it that it is actually safe. It is this introduction of the reality of safety, that actually unravels the state and heals the system.

> **Simply 'allowing' the system to
> react without suppression,
> demonstrates that you have
> become safe. That is enough
> for it to heal!**

If you picture something you really want, or something you really don't want it will trigger emotional, mental, and even physical reactions. Remember, the nervous system cannot tell the difference between a real and an imagined threat. They both trigger the same response mechanism.

I know this isn't easy. In fact, it is very difficult to sit with uncomfortable feelings, but, this is how it is done. It is the Tao. The **only** way.

What is really amazing is that once you actually do it, once you turn inward and allow it to be the way that it is, the healing begins immediately.

> *The resistance that keeps us from even beginning this work is actually way more painful than the work itself*

Remember, the resistant state is resistant to doing inner work. It does not want to be exposed. The work is easy... getting to the work is where the real challenge lies.

Chapter 13
Mastery & Your Natural State

"We talk of our mastery of nature, which sounds very grand; but the fact is we respectfully adapt ourselves, first, to her ways." - Clarence Day

The Law of Attraction gurus are right. You DO have to learn to 'Allow', but almost nobody can do it on their own. No, I take that back. NOBODY can do it on their own. Even the world's greatest athletes have coaches that work with them every day, even when they are already superstars.

So, just telling you to allow is not enough. You have to be shown how, guided, and supported until you get it!

'Allowing' is NOT a quick fix. It is serious training.

To provide that training is the reason I created the "Just Allow It" audio and video course. It consists of seven hours of audio exercises, about five hours of video training, a membership site, a Facebook community, and regular support calls. It is a complete program for mastering this art.

'Allowing', like any worthwhile endeavor, requires a lot of practice before it is mastered. After all, you have been trained into resistance almost from the beginning of your life, and maybe even before that! It shouldn't be any big shock that it might take some time to retrain the system into the 'Tao Of Allowing'.

But, like any skill, given good training, practice, patience, and consistency, it can be mastered. Remember, allowing isn't second nature - it's first.

It may not seem that way, because we have lost touch with it but..

Allowing is really a return to normalcy

It is a return to our real self, and, because it really is your natural state, it is way easier to master, than, say, playing the piano, or tightrope walking. And so, I can pretty much guarantee that you will see immediate shifts in your attitude, your behavior, and your life, right from the beginning.

We are really just returning to what has been innate in us all along. We are just coming home.

What, No Bounce?

I often compare it to a rubber ball. Take a nice round rubber ball and squeeze it tightly. It goes out of shape, of course, and, being out of shape, it can't bounce. It can't roll. It really isn't much of a ball at all. It may even go to ball therapy and have cosmetic ball surgery.

It will go to visualization seminars and study the Law of Bounce-a-Traction. But it won't make any difference. It may even give up and say, "Bouncing and rolling works for everybody else. But not for me."

What really has to happen is that that tight, unrelenting grip has to be released. We have to let go of the squeezing. Notice what happens then. Once the grip has been released, the ball springs back into its original shape. Its natural resiliency causes it to become whole again. Spontaneously. Effortlessly. It does not even need a period of convalescence or physical therapy. It immediately returns to its natural form.

So it is with balls. So it is with us. So it is with you.

Chapter 14
Who You REALLY Are

"It takes courage to grow up and become who you really are." - e. e. cummings

As you may have noticed, I have used the phrase "who you really are" several times in this book. "And just who might that be?" you may be wondering.

I have said repeatedly that who you really are was expressed as a child, and, when that expression met with the disapproval of The Tribe, that quality or aspect of your being was suppressed. It was quite literally sent to the basement.

Who you are is the sum total of all of those qualities which were built into your from the beginning.

Who you are is all of those inherent qualities that belong to you and you alone

It is the sum total of all those qualities, and much, much more.

I can't point to a particular thing and say, "that's you!" I can't point to a particular quality or even entire groups of qualities. The wonder of being is the simple fact that there is nothing in particular you can point at, and say, "That is me."

You are too vast, too subtle, and have too much of a range of expression for that.

You are the potential for anything

Yet everything you do, say, think, and feel, does have a particular quality about it. A certain, indefinable something that is totally unique. That indefinable, ineffable quality is you. *You Are That!*

Now, please do not go trying to define it. You can't. Don't try to put the whole thing in a box and come up with some story or idea. Stories, concepts, ideas, interpretations, explanations, all fall miserably short.

This makes the whole mystery of it even more delicious! It is even too big for your mind to grasp. Are you ready for this? You can't **know** who you are. There is no thought that could possibly contain you.

You can't KNOW who you are - You can only BE who you are

But, far from leaving you in the dark of unknowing, this mystery makes everyday a discovery. Every day becomes a treasure hunt. Instead of life being a series of accomplishments or goals, it becomes a perpetual unfoldment. You never reach an endpoint and declare, "oh , THAT is who I am!" Instead, it is simply a, "wow! I am THAT too? Cool!"

And there is one final bit of really good news. There is nothing you need to do to be what you already are, and there is nothing you can do to stop it! To fully be yourself, and express that infinite something, is your destiny.

The 'Tao Of Allowing' is the key to realizing that destiny, and settling in to what you have always been.

My dear, dear friend. Welcome home!

Conclusion?

Great accomplishment seems imperfect,

Yes it does not outlive its usefulness

Great fullness seems empty,

Yet it cannot be exhausted

- Lao Tsu

The Tao of Allowing

There is no conclusion to the Tao. Life is infinite in nature, and is forever creating new vistas of beauty and purpose, and so, mastery never concludes. It never ends. The real master is the perpetual student. The master's mind is the beginner's mind. The childlike delight of continuous discovery is the master's joy. We never really know. We only continually discover.

As you will hear me say over and over again, "to study the Law of Attraction is to study yourself." There is no end to this study because there is no end to you, nor are there any limits on your nature, on what you are capable of, or, on your ability to enjoy, to surf, to flow, to love and to be loved.

Everything you consider "negative" in your life is actually not negative at all. It is merely being interpreted as negative by your resistant state. It got colored as negative as a strategy of suppression. Even a great opportunity will be called negative and regarded with suspicion when viewed from a resistant state.

But the resistant state is only a program in the nervous system. It is NOT you! It is not your nature. It is not a flaw in your character, or a defect in your soul. It isn't you at all. It is a defensive posture and nothing else.

The system *wants* to be free of it. Yes, it *wants* to. It knows that it is not its natural state, but it will not let go until it is convinced that you are safe. It isn't even doing this for itself, it is doing it for you. It is your job to convince it that you are safe, and, once you do, it will take care of the rest.

I hope you will take this practice on and free your body from all of its imaginary fears. They were not imaginary at one time, but they are now. That is what we have to be willing to show it, and we accomplish that by mastering the 'Tao Of Allowing'.

Benediction

Let me leave you with this: Imagine life without struggle, without fear, without conflict, and without doubt. Really. Stop and imagine.

We have become so habituated into this state of resistance that we oftentimes won't even let ourselves imagine such a thing. We assume that there will always be fear, doubt, concern, worry, resistance, defensiveness. We assume that that is the way it must be.

It most definitely is *not!*

Freedom from all of that is not only possible, it is your birthright. It is your destiny. It is why you are here. That State of Allowing (a.k.a. freedom) does not need to be acquired, it only needs to be discovered. It is, after all, the realty of your being.

> *"Having never left the house, you are asking for the way home."* -
> **Nisargadatta Maharaj**

Yes, it has been covered up by artificial behaviors, beliefs, attitudes, and patterns of reaction that have obscured it, *but it is still there.* Clouds block the sun, but they can't extinguish it, and it is exactly so for you.

So I invite you, with all my heart, to begin to explore the 'Tao Of Allowing' for yourself. To begin to discover that you are way more than you ever thought you were. To give yourself the greatest gift that could ever be given. To simply 'allow' yourself to be who you are, who you have always been, and to discover that that is all you have ever wanted.

Be yourself and be happy. This is the **'Tao Of Allowing'**.

My Gift To You...

I want you to continue on this road to mastery. So...

I am going to give you the Body Awareness exercise from my "Just Allow It!" course!

The basic 'Body Awareness' is the very first exercise that the course teaches, and it is an extended version of the exercise I walked you though at the beginning of the book. It is much longer, contains music and atmosphere, and I guide you through with my voice.

I really want you to experience this, master it, and share it. I will take you through the exercise. I will be Dad running next to you while you get the hang of it. Just head back over to the same page *http://JustAllowIt.net/TaoOfAllowing*. You can download it, put it on your iPod or Smartphone and give it a go.

I can't wait to hear about the effect it has on your sense of well-being and how that gets reflected in your life.

About the Author

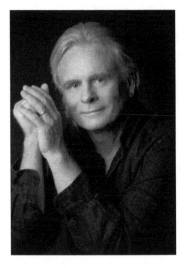

GP Walsh is a spiritual teacher, author, speaker, personal and professional coach, personal growth facilitator, and workshop leader living in Miami Beach in the US. He is recognized as a true Master Coach, Master Meditation teacher and Expert in Energy Healing using the Emotional Freedom Technique (EFT).

He is the author of the "Just Allow It$^{\circledR}$" Audio/Video Course, The "Law of Attraction 2.0" Video Course, "the 7 Eyes of the Soul", "Tapping on the Buddha", "The Oneness Experience" "Negative Emotions Are A Self-Help Myth" and the upcoming book "The Vision with The Purpose Process."

He has been teaching and healing for over 30 years and has helped literally thousands of people move towards richer and more fulfilling lives. Lives that are not merely successful but are filled with meaning, purpose and spirituality.

In addition to his writing and his courses, he gives talks and workshops both live and via the Internet.

He also has a weekly radio show called "Law of Attraction 2.0 - Spiritual Straight Talk" (http://LOA20.com) where he answers any and all questions about any subject related to personal and spiritual growth. The show is syndicated through the Law of Attraction Radio network (http://LOARadioNetwork.com/gpwalsh) and heard by over 20,000 people in 120 countries every month.

Resources

GP's main website http://GPWalsh.com

Law of Attraction 2.0 - http://LOA20.com

The Vision - With The Purpose Process

7 Eyes of the Soul

Tapping on the Buddha - Using EFT for Self-Discovery and Spiritual Growth

'Just Allow It' Audio/Video Course http://JustAllowIt.net

The Law of Attraction 2.0 Audio/Video Course

The Balls Project - Self Help For Men http://BallsProject.com

Clear Mind Sound - Audio Meditations and Brain Entrainment http://ClearMindSound.com

All of the resources mention in this book:

- The audio book

- The audio exercises

The Tao of Allowing

- The free Just Allow It Body Awareness exercise

- The diagrams

- The video series "There Is NO Unconscious Mind!"

Can all be found at

http://JustAllowIt.net/TaoOfAllowing

Made in the USA
Middletown, DE
26 June 2015